God's Communicators in Mission

EUGENE W. BUNKOWSKE
and
RICHARD FRENCH

A Booklet of Essays
Delivered At The
Third Annual
Missions Congress

Concordia Theological Seminary
Fort Wayne, Indiana
September 30 – October 2, 1987

CONTENTS

PREFACE

Concordia Theological Seminary recognizes that God's Message and God's Great Commission to be sent-ones is central to all that ministerial training is about. It therefore has responded positively and dynamically to the 1979 call of the Lutheran Church-Missouri Synod's Synodical Convention to adopt the Mission Challenges of the 1980's by offering "necessary mission courses . . . and curricular and co-curricular mission activities in order to develop an all-pervasive mission vision and outreach."

The Annual Mission Congress is a response to the Church's call for action in the area of Mission education but, at an even deeper level, it is a response to the basic missionary nature of Christianity. This Congress is dedicated to the cause of bringing together, on a yearly basis, speakers and participants who are committed to the missionary nature of Christianity, that is, people who are on the cutting edge of exemplifying Christian witness and outreach in their lives and of articulating it in ways that communicate positively to our world.

A second goal of the Mission Congress is to work toward developing a body of high quality oral, written, and video material that can serve as a solid basis for missionary education, including motivation, commitment, and training.

Dr. Eugene W. Bunkowske
Director of Missions and
Chairman, Pastoral Ministries
Department

Dr. Robert Preus
President
Concordia Theological
Seminary

FOREWORD

The Third Annual Missions Congress was held at Concordia Theological Seminary, Ft. Wayne, Indiana, from September 30 to October 2, 1987, taking as its theme "God's Communicators in Mission." The purpose of the Congress was to deepen the understanding of pastors and lay people of how God has communicated His message of salvation in Christ to man and to awaken the interest of pastors and laity in being God's communicators of the message to others, especially across cultural lines. As last year, there was an average attendance at each session of 170 people; registrants came from 13 states and Canada.

The present booklet is a result of this conference. The essays and sermons concentrate on cross-cultural communication of the Gospel from varying points of view, and yet together they form a unified whole. A glance at the Table of Contents will indicate both the unity and diversity of this volume. The editors feel certain that "God's Communicators in Mission" will be of interest not only to those who attended the conference and participated in it, but also to students and faculty involved in Missions courses at Christian high schools, colleges, and seminaries, to mission boards of local churches, and to any reader with an interest in improving his skills as a communicator of God's Word in our varied world.

Along with the papers printed in this booklet, the LCMS Board for Mission Services staff with guests Mr. Robert Law and Rev. John Shep presented reports covering fifteen mission subjects under the title "God's Messengers in Action" on Wednesday afternoon, September 30. The reports dealt with these topics: Black ministry, rural ministry, handicapped ministry, campus ministry, Hispanic ministry, urban ministry, U. S. Asian ministry, church planting, spreading the Gospel behind the Iron

Curtain, ministry through print, Laborers for Christ, and ministry to the Armed Forces.

There were also field reports on Africa, Asia, and Latin America. In addition, The Rev. James Likens presented a series of videos on Thursday, October 1 concerning mission outreach in the United States and abroad. The titles of these videos were "How Will They Know?," "Hymn of Celebration of Change," "Big Joe," "Salifu's Harvest," and "Whom Shall I Send?" Pastor Likens, who serves a parish in Indianapolis, prepared these videos himself with the help of the Board for Mission Services.

As you can easily imagine, many people contributed to the success of the Third Annual Missions Congress. The editors would like to acknowledge some of them now. The vision and leadership of Drs. Preus and Bunkowske continued to inspire everyone involved. Bob Marshall took over the responsibility of General Coordinator in planning and organizing the details of the Congress. Mr. Elmer Eggen and the volunteers in the Great Commission Resource Library again assisted in a number of important ways, including preparation of the bulk mailing; Sharon France saw to the day-to-day correspondence and other details; Cheryl Marshall and Doris Bowman handled the registration and accounting and organized prayer support. Joel Brandvold supervised videotaping each presentation, while Randy Baird and Gary Grossman handled audiotaping. Robert Roberts took care of publicity and also helped with the production of this booklet. Madalene Eggold and Cheryl Marshall transcribed some of the presentations so that we could include them here. An anonymous donor made the publication of this material possible with a generous contribution. We thank all of them for their efforts.

CAMERON A. MacKENZIE

Prof. MacKenzie is an assistant professor in the departments of Historical and Exegetical Theology at Concordia Theological Seminary and serves as Director of Library Services. Before joining the faculty in 1983, he served St. Matthew Lutheran Church in Detroit, Michigan, as pastor (1975-83) and as headmaster of its school (1972-83), where he was actively engaged in evangelizing the unreached—Arabs, Hispanics, low income, etc. Prof. MacKenzie received his A. B. from the University of Detroit, an M. A. in history from the University of Chicago, an M. A. in classics from Wayne State University, and an S.T.M. in New Testament from Concordia, Fort Wayne. His major interest is the English Reformation and Puritanism. Prof. MacKenzie and his wife, Meg, along with their three children live at 6 Tyndale Place, Ft. Wayne.

"CROSS-CULTURAL" IS
FOR EVERYBODY

A Sermon Preached by Prof. Cameron A. MacKenzie
on October 1, 1987
Text: 1 Corinthians 9:19-23

Can you imagine a more extraordinary career? From Pharisee of the Pharisees to cross-cultural missionary, from meticulous observation of all Jewish laws and customs to rubbing shoulders and breaking bread with vile pagans, from the rabbi, Saul of Tarsus, to the apostle, St. Paul, of the Christian Church. It's mind-boggling. As a young man, Paul was so careful to eat just what the Jewish law prescribed, so careful not to incur ritual defilement by association with Gentiles, so careful to keep the Jewish Sabbath—not just out of habit or custom but for reasons of conscience, out of obedience to the God who had made such laws; and yet later on, he gave it all up—the peculiar food, dress, and laws—in order to associate easily and freely with all kinds of non-Jews, ranging from Athenian intellectuals on Mars Hill to the gross pagans of Lystra who thought he was the god Mercury.

And at what personal cost Paul made this change! He had been the fair-haired boy of Jerusalem's Pharisees—a disciple of the great Gamaliel, full of zeal and enthusiasm for the cause; in fact, so talented and dedicated was Paul that when the leadership looked about for someone to entrust with the extirpation of the new Christian heresy they chose Paul and even granted him authority to extend his persecuting work into Damascus. Yes, Paul was their man—he had the right background, the right education, and the right dedication for keeping Judaism the way the Pharisees liked it—pure and separate from all alien influences—and therefore, within this circle, Paul's future seemed secure.

But when Paul kicked over the traces to enter the camp of the Christians, we must admit that his career immediately went down hill, for not only did he have to travel thereafter and give up all hope of normal family life, not only did he have to associate with all kinds of people that by previous training he must have found repulsive, he also had to suffer rejection, alienation, and persecution from his erstwhile friends the Jews *and* from his new-found cause the Gentiles. Beaten, scourged, stoned, almost drowned, hounded by enemies from one place to the next, misunderstood by friends, betrayed by those whom he loved, until at last we find him at the end virtually alone, awaiting death at the hands of Roman authorities. It sounds harsh to say it but from a worldly point of view, Paul was a loser, a failure.

And yet in the words of our text, Paul seems to be holding himself forth as an example, i.e., if you and I also claim to follow Jesus, then we too should be ready to surrender our past, our ways and customs, indeed our freedom to be what we want to be in order to reach people with Paul's message about Christ.

Now, there's a lot within me that rebels at a text like this. In fact when it was first assigned me, I did not want to preach on it—because I don't want to accommodate myself to all kinds of people the way Paul did. In fact, by temperament I'm much more comfortable with the Pharisees than with the cross-cultural types—I like things to stay the same. So my first thought was to restrict this text to missionaries or would-be missionaries, where of course the application is obvious. As in Paul's case, to prove effective, a missionary has to adjust to the people he's trying to reach with his message—has to learn their language, their ways and customs, and so establish a bond of understanding and trust between himself and the people so that they will listen to his word when he speaks it.

Upon reflection, however, it seems clear that the same considerations must also apply to the clergy in general—not just the ones who stay put right here in the United States: good pastors, effective pastors, are sensitive to cultural barriers that separate them even partially from their people and seek to penetrate those barriers. Ethnicity and race are, of course, obvious ones; but so are education and taste, even interests and hobbies. Let me cite just a few examples: the inner city pastor who commutes from the suburbs, or the rural pastor who takes no interest in the price of grain, or the Detroit pastor who drives a Toyota, or the Chicago pastor who roots for the New York Mets—all are making the mistake of failing to identify as closely as possible with the people they serve.

Now, certainly, from one point of view such things are trivial, and most people can accommodate the cultural eccentricities of their shepherds. However, it is very easy for the trivial to become significant when people begin to see such differences as signs of pride or manifestations of feelings of superiority on the part of their pastors—and as soon as that happens, they erect an enormous wall between themselves and the one they call "pastor": they lose respect for him, they find fault with him, and they talk about him—not about his message but about him. In fact, the message becomes almost irrelevant when people believe that their pastor is not one with them, for they interpret his words as those of a hypocrite—how can he preach about the law of God when he doesn't love them? Paul's words in our text apply to all pastors, not just missionaries.

But do they apply to all Christians, clergy and laity alike? Do they speak to believers who have no desire at all to become clergy? Certainly, they do, for the same things that can separate pastor from people can also separate people from one another. Just think how difficult it has been, for example, for the parishes of our large cities to survive when the neighborhood has changed from white to black or from Anglo to Hispanic or from middle-class German-American to almost anything else: finances have dried up, numbers have dwindled, and the doors of churches have closed. Why? Certainly not for any lack of people to tell about Jesus nor because other ethnic groups won't respond to the Gospel. No—the problem is class, culture, customs. Unfortunately, too many church people are like me—comfortable with the way things are and with people like ourselves and therefore resistant to doing what it takes to overcome the things that divide us from others for the sake of reaching them with the Gospel.

But that's certainly not the word or example of St. Paul, is it? However, is St. Paul's word or example reason enough for changing the way we behave and inconveniencing ourselves to reach others different from ourselves? I don't think so: it certainly wasn't enough for Paul—who sought not to please himself but someone else. Let's go back to that career story as we sketched it before and realize that the transformation in Paul took place in the first instance outside of Paul, i.e., Jesus Christ appeared to Paul and changed him from Pharisee to apostle.

Apart from the reality of Jesus Christ crucified and risen again, Paul's life and career make no sense at all—they defy rational explanation. But when we realize that the Lord Himself appeared to Paul, convicted and converted him, then what the apostle did with the rest of his life seems almost inevitable, for Christ had freed him from a horrible burden, an actual slavery, to observing the smallest particulars of traditional law. Furthermore, Paul was laboring under the enormous weight of sin: the pride, the cruelty, the murder, the blasphemy that had characterized his "successful" life were only taken away by Christ's cross and washed away in baptism. Therefore, having experienced God's grace for him and knowing that forgiveness, life, and heaven were his eternally, Paul freely surrendered his time, talents, tastes, and predilections to the service of Christ and His Gospel. And that is why we should do the same—not for Paul but for Jesus.

If the barriers of race, language, culture and the like sometimes seem too great for us to overcome and we'd prefer just to hunker down content with our own little worlds, let's remember what barriers Christ had to overcome in order to save us. Since human beings were at risk, Christ became a human being, God became flesh, the Creator became creature. Then, since it was God's law that demanded obedience, Christ humbled Himself in order to obey that law, even though that meant submitting to human needs and emotions as well as to the whims of other human beings. Thus, He who made all things hungered and thirsted; He who could do all things became tired and slept; He who ruled all things obeyed parents, teachers, governors. Furthermore, since God's justice demanded payment for sins, Christ did that, too: He suffered and died; the Prince of Life yielded up His life to save those who had freely chosen death. Therefore, when at last our Lord burst from the tomb, He was breaking through all the seemingly insurmountable barriers separating God from man; but not one thing—not humanity nor the law nor sin nor death— would the Savior permit to stand between God and man. In

Christ, Paul, you, I, everybody has a gracious God, a heavenly Father: we are one in Him and one with each other.

In a sense, therefore, when we accommodate ourselves to others for the sake of the Gospel, we are only realizing visibly the reality that Christ has already accomplished, viz., our oneness in Him. When we learn another language in order to preach God's Word or live next to someone of another race in order to share the Gospel or simply welcome a stranger into our congregation, we are embracing a brother in Christ—we are saying that what Jesus has done for him and me renders all differences between us meaningless, superficial, indeed nothing. It still may not be *easy* for us to be all things to all men, and we will always be imperfect in our efforts and accomplishments—but it can be done by missionaries, pastors, and laity alike on the basis of what Christ has done already for us. "This I do for the Gospel's sake," said St. Paul, "that I might be a partaker thereof with you."

When the Pharisee of the Jews became the apostle to the Gentiles he appeared to be joining the losing side; and even when he died, though he left little bands of followers throughout the Mediterranean basin, his executioners would hardly have recognized him as a great success. In spite of appearances, however, God had used Paul to save some—indeed countless numbers—through the end of time by his powerful pen.

Of course, none of us here is another St. Paul; but God will also use us for His work. We may never really see the fruits of our labors, but we can be confident that God is still saving some when the Gospel tears down barriers: between us and each other, between us and others, between us and God. Amen.

CARL F. H. HENRY

Dr. Henry has had a varied and distinguished career as theologian, author, editor, teacher, and lecturer. He received a B. A. from Wheaton College in 1938, a Th. D. from Northern Baptist Theological Seminary in 1942, and a Ph. D. from Boston University in 1949. He was founding editor of *Christianity Today,* which he served in editorial capacities from 1956-74. He has served on the faculty at Northern Baptist Theological Seminary, Fuller Theological Seminary, and Eastern Baptist Seminary. He has lectured at numerous campuses both in America and abroad and has received three honorary degrees. In 1966, he was chairman of the World Congress on Evangelism in Berlin. He has written 35 books, including *Remaking the Modern Mind, Aspects of Christian Social Ethics,* and he has completed a six-volume work called *God, Revelation, and Authority.*

THE CROWNED CHRIST
AND HIS COURAGEOUS CHURCH

Carl F. H. Henry, Th. D. Ph. D.

"You shall receive power when the Holy Spirit has come upon you; and you shall be witnesses to Me in Jerusalem in all Judea and Samaria, and to the end of the earth" (Acts 1:8).

If the church is really going to count for much today amid the emptiness of modern life, we shall need to regain the momentum and joy of the first Christians. For the contemporary church has lost much of the radiance of the Christian beginnings; the luster is gone. We know the glow of Easter Sunday, but we lack the post-Easter afterglow.

Why has this happened? Has it not occurred largely because we are caught up in the lust for things? We are trapped by the materialistic ambitions of our age. We think that more of this world's goods is what will make us truly happy. Even some clergy seem to think that more financial support is all one needs in order to guarantee the success of their programs.

For years I have travelled and ministered in and out of the Third World, most recently in Romania, that repressive Communist nation in Eastern Europe. There are long breadlines and meatlines; supplies are meager and are quickly exhausted. Christians are discriminated against; they are kept from management jobs because they are identified with the Church rather than with the Communist party. Yet Christians in Romania have a sense of holy joy that our congregations often lack. Why is it that Christians in a Communist police state can know the deep reality and presence of God, much as did the early Christians in the totalitarian Roman empire, while we with our wonted freedom to worship God and our possessions are so spiritually empty and joyless? Did they know something that we do not know? What was the secret of their devotion? The West has an abundance of this world's things, but it has little joy. The accumulation of material things sucks our spirits dry.

The reason for this is that the early Christians lived in the real world. We live in artificial worlds. The real world is not the world postulated by horoscopes and ruled by the stars. It is not a world determined by economic forces and moving relentlessly, as Marxists think, toward Communist revolution. It is not Carl Sagan's *Cosmos* reducible to impersonal processes and quantum events. It is not the natural universe on which contemporary economists concentrate; it is not the world of material things. That world is passing away; it has no real durability. It offers no real joy or security.

I don't mean that the world in which we live is an illusion in the sense that Buddhists and Hindus maintain, a mere appearance of the Brahma-All or the Buddha-All. But it is not the ultimately real world. The real world is the world in which God lives, in which the eternal Christ lives, in which Abraham and Isaiah invested their hearts and lives, and of which the Gospels and Epistles tell us. It is the world in which eternal life reigns, the world from which the incarnate Jesus came and in which the Risen Jesus even now exercises his high priestly ministry and hears and answers the prayers of believers.

The Church finds her true self-identity and mission only in that context; without the supernatural realities the Church soon loses power and joy and her reason for being. I ask you therefore whether you live in the real world today, whether you are spiritually alive; whether Christ has made you whole; whether the Holy Spirit is filling you daily; whether God possesses your mind and heart? Do we live as the early Christians did in the ultimately real world?

For one thing, the early Christians knew that *the crowned Christ above creates his Church below.*

They knew that the Church is not a material building located at an intersection of two streets to which people optionally commute to hear a professional lecturer speak for 20 or 25 minutes, and where, at a given signal, they drop a bill in the collection to keep a roof on the building and to subsidize denominational statistics. They knew the Church as a new society of the redeemed, as a fellowship of spiritually reborn sinners, whose life is supernatural.

They knew that a heavenly voice had called the Church into being, the resurrection voice of Him who said, "I am he that liveth and was dead" (Rev 1:18).

The disciples knew not only Jesus' earthly ministry: his wonderful words—the discourses, the parables—and his unforgettable works or miracles and signs. Stunned as they were by his crucifixion, they were shocked alive by his resurrection from the dead. He who said, "It is finished" said "handle me and see that it is I myself;" He who gave up the Spirit on Golgotha breathed the Holy Spirit on them. Saul of Tarsus heard that voice on the Damascus Road: "Saul, Saul, why persecutest thou *Me*?"

They knew that the risen Christ was calling His Church into being. The most dramatic aspect of their gathering, as we do here, was the invisible presence and activity of the Risen Head of the Church among them. Their gathering was no routine matter, for He had promised that "where two or three were gathered in my name, there shall I be in the midst of them." Are you aware that the crucified Carpenter of Nazareth, the Risen Jesus, is present with us and is personally active in our midst? "He touched me," they said to one another, and to their families and friends. The Risen Jesus had met with them, and was calling his Church into being.

They knew Jesus not only as risen, but as ascended also.

Once it seemed that the Father had spurned Him: "My God, my God, why hast *Thou* forsaken *Me*?" But then He "was taken up" into heaven, or as the King James version has it, He was "received up." The Father was waiting to receive Him and welcomed Him on high. The sinless one who bore our sins and propitiated the wrath of God ascended to the Father.

That ascension changed their life and outlook. They turned their praise to the ascended Lord. They lifted their prayers to the ascended Lord. They proclaimed the ascended Lord and they obeyed the ascended Lord.

What difference does His ascension make in your life and ministry? For the early Christians, the ascension of Jesus was a pledge of their own coming rapture. "Whither the forerunner is *for us* entered" (Heb 6:20), writes the author of Hebrews. Jesus' ascension signaled sunrise for their own souls; the prospect of being in God's very presence had dawned.

They knew Jesus not only as risen and ascended, but as exalted also.

He, the Head of the Church, sat down at the Father's right hand. They knew Christ on the throne—not merely the Christ of the Bethlehem manger, of the Sermon on the Mount, of the Gethsemane garden, of Golgotha, of the Empty Tomb, of the Emmaus way, and of ascension morning. They knew the "crowned Christ." They knew that the ministry from Galilee to Golgotha had given way to a new ministry, that of Christ the High Priest, ministering from the throne of God.

They knew that the universe is not ultimately in the grip of totalitarian Caesars or of blind fate or of Satan and demonic forces or of impersonal processes and Big Bang contingencies. The author of Hebrews writes: "We see not yet all things under Him, but we see Jesus"—Jesus in his dominion over death, over sin and Satan, over nature and history.

They knew that the crowned Christ was calling his Church into being. They were not just part of a holy succession, of a sacred tradition. They knew that the Crowned Christ had given them new being and a new fellowship. *"He* added to the church daily such as should be saved," says Acts 2:47. "He gave some to be apostles, prophets, evangelists, pastors, and teachers," writes Paul (Eph 4:11).

They knew that the Crowned Christ was creating His Church below—in Judea, and Asia, and Europe, and unto the uttermost parts. The Crowned Christ above creates His Church below.

They knew more than this. They knew not only that the crowned Christ above creates his Church below, they knew that *the crowned Christ above commissions his church below.* Just as the Church received her life from outside herself, from the transcendant order through the Risen Christ, now ascended and glorified, so too they knew that the Church received· her very direction, her vocation, her mission on the face of the earth from the Risen Jesus, that the Great Commission had fallen from Resurrection lips. That fact marked off the church and still does from every human enterprise, however commendable, however humanitarian in nature, they may be. The Risen Lord himself gave the Church her marching orders. Great visions of social ethics have come to us from Plato and Aristotle and others, including the world-engulfing programs of Alexander and the Caesars and of Hitler and Marx. But the Church's mission was given by One who rose from the dead after public crucifixion. The commission "Go ye into all the world and preach the Gospel unto all nations" was enunciated by a Resurrection voice.

This world-mission of the Church was not just an accidental turn of events. The disciples, the Apostles themselves, may have been somewhat unsure of their task, even during the forty days after the Resurrection and before His ascension. They say to Jesus, "Lord, wilt Thou at this time restore again the Kingdom to Israel?" (Acts 1:6). They bulked all their expectations on Jesus Christ alone, and what he would do, and they saw the future through the prospect of political restoration. "Wilt thou at this time restore again the kingdom to Israel?" And Jesus said, "It is not for you to know the times and the seasons which the Father has in His own control. *You* shall receive power, the Holy Spirit coming upon you, and you shall be witnesses unto Me in Jerusalem and Judea and Samaria and unto the uttermost part of the world" (Acts 1:8). "Go ye into all the world...."—and in that "go ye" the mission of the Church was born; by it the Church's distinctive task in the world was indicated. It turned them from merely regional witnesses, as once He had sent them out two by two as the twelve, two by two as the seventy for a regional witness of short duration, he turned them loose with a global mission, geographically unlimited and not of temporal duration, but to be the task of the Church throughout the years of her existence until the Lord Himself would return.

"As the Father has sent Me into the world, even so send I you" (John 20:21), said Jesus. The great British commentator B. F. Westcott remarked that Jesus integrated them and us into the redemption covenant of the Godhead. As the Father sent the Son, so the Son has sent us. The Church of Christ was not to be at ease in Zion, but "on the march;" she was to be scattered throughout the world empires, bearing witness to her Commander in Chief; she was to tell of the resurrection of the crucified Jesus who spurs the Church onward in the fulfillment of this mission and emboldens believers where obedience carries risks.

"Go ye!" said Jesus. We say that the circumstances are against it. But God is the God of circumstances. He is the Lord of providence. The early Christians knew that it is necessary to obey God rather than man. They had one supreme fear, that they would fail Christ in their appointed mission. In some countries today the believer is exposed to government hostility and intimidation and bears witness at the risk of work penalties. We have incomparable freedom to bear witness, and yet we are intimidated by peer pressures. I sat this morning next to an Air Force service man and I wondered if I should speak to him about Christ, until I recalled that three weeks ago I was in Romania, in a full church of people standing along the sides and seated in front and filling the galleries and overflowing into the pastor's study leading off from the pulpit. My translator was a scientist who'd been converted and who could never have a management job because he was not a member of the Communist Party and was taking lower wages because he wasn't getting advancement. He worked with fellow-scientists and he would occasionally put in his papers which had to be shared with other scientists passages that he had written out like Paul's statement in Romans about the heavens, the eternal power and deity of God manifest in the Creation and the heavens declare the glory of God from Psalm 19. One day he said to one of the women-scientists who was working near him whether she had perhaps found some papers in her notes and she said to him loudly, "Don't you ever talk to me about God again! Don't you know that every intelligent person knows there is no God?" And others scientists who were in the room heard this and got in on a devil's advocate basis, and one said, "How can anyone say for sure that there is no God," and they got into a discussion about this. That night, in the service in which this translator was translating for me, that woman scientist who had become a Christian in the previous weeks was in the congregation; she'd hoped to bring her husband, who was another scientist and she said to me after the service, "We are praying for him. It will take a little time, but he will come." So there are *risks* in witness and where there are risks, people are risking it and they are finding the holy joy of God as the early Christians did.

The early Christians knew that the Crowned Christ above commissions his Church below; that He is a co-worker in the fulfillment of our evangelistic assignment: "The work that I do shall ye do also" (John 14:12). Have we heard the divine commission for ourselves—not as something enunciated by a theological professor or by a pastor, but by the exalted Lord, who commisions His church below.

Not only does the Crowned Christ above create His church below, not only does the Crowned Christ above commission his church below, *but the Crowned Christ above confirms His Church below.* The crucified and ascended Lord lifts us to new relationships, to new virtues, and to new power.

First, to new relationships. The early Christians knew the triune God living in their hearts. "If a man loves me, he will keep my word," said Jesus, "and my Father will love him, and we will come to him and abide with him" (John 14:23). The Father and the Son make their home with us and in us. "Christ in you the glorious hope," Paul writes to the Colossians (1:27). By and through the Holy Spirit, the Father and the Son dwell in us. The Spirit, said Jesus, would dwell with us forever (John 14:16 ff.). "Don't you know," Paul asks the Corinthians, "That your bodies are the temples of the living God?" (1 Cor 3:16). The entire Godhead is implicated in the Christian life. We who were aliens to God are privileged participants in a circle of spiritual relationships linking the Father, the Son, and the Spirit to us and us to the Father, the Son, and the Spirit. The exalted Christ confirms His church by lifting us to new relationships.

Secondly, we are lifted to new virtues. The ascended Jesus who is head of the Church has already passed through death and resurrection and is alive forever in the eternal order. From the eternities, through the Spirit whom He first poured out at Pentecost, He bestows upon the Church virtues that belong to the age to come. "We have an earnest of our inheritance," Paul writes (Eph 1:14). The fruit of the Spirit is "love, joy, peace, patience, kindness, goodness, faithfulness, gentleness, self-control" (Gal 5:22 ff.). We are to be filled daily with the Holy Spirit of God, manifesting in and to the world the distinctive Christian virtues. Christ gives his disciples a peace that the world cannot give. He exhibits an incomparable love, and He exhorts us to love even as He loved—to love the Father, to love the saints, to love the lost and lead them to eternal life.

Among the new virtues to which Christ lifts His Church is joy; it appears second only to love on Paul's agenda. The pagans of antiquity were joyless; the nonchristian world was in the grip of melancholy. Joy does not even appear as a virtue in the writings of the moral philosophers of antiquity. But the great philosopher Augustine was first attracted to Christians by their spontaneous joy. Christians know what true joy is because they know not only this world of things that is passing away, but the eternal world from which we experience eternal life, a life fit for eternity, a life of virtue that the Risen Jesus exemplified and that the ascended Lord nurtures. We are lifted to new virtues.

Third, we are lifted to new power. We have already spoken of new moral power in respect to the virtues. But the power potential to which we are related is even more comprehensive and awesome. It is important to mention this in a day when political power and scientific power so much preoccupy the modern world that the secular mind thinks God has been eclipsed. We speak of the superpowers as if they were the acme of power, and of nuclear power as if it held captive the fortunes of humanity. Sometimes even Christians seem intimidated—as if we can refer to God almighty only apologetically in a world that dialogues about the Big Bang or about nuclear missiles and strategic defense initiatives. But the early Christians would have seen no reason to be intimidated by these historical developments, awesome as they are. They knew that God is the eternal Superpower and that Jesus Christ is the King of kings and the Lord of lords. Neither man-made power nor the great world powers were to be compared to El Shaddai, God Almighty; the all-powerful Creator reminds the whole human race in all the generations of history of His "eternal power and deity" (Rom 1:20). That is what Paul writes the Christians in Rome, the seat of the great world empire of that day, the place from which the Caesars reigned. "Ever since the beginning of the world," he writes, God has in and through the creation manifested the "eternal power and divinity." There is *power* supreme: the Creator of all, the preserver of all, the moral judge of all, the final judge of men and nations. The early Christians were on speaking terms with the ultimate and all-powerful One. They knew the Lord of life—creation life, redemption life, resurrection life; the One who has the power of life and death, who has triumphed over sin and death and who can make all things new. The early Christians knew that the Risen Lord has lifted us to a new order of life in which evil is doomed and good will triumph and that the decisive victory in this cosmic struggle has already taken place on crucifixion-resurrection weekend.

About the incomparable divine power they knew even more. They knew that nothing can separate the believer from the almighty love and power of God. The Romans vaunted their world power; they were conquerors. But Paul reminds the believers that they are "more than conquerors;" they are in fact super-conquerors, who stand beyond devastating defeat. It was centuries before the fall and sack of Rome, but the seeds of destruction were already at work, as Gibbon indicates in *The Decline and Fall of the Roman Empire.* Paul describes these moral and spiritual failures with precision. The world powers build not only on weak foundations but on wrong foundations. But the Christian is linked to God whose power conquers sin and death, and nothing can separate us from God's love—neither death nor life, nor angels nor principalities nor powers, nor things present nor things to come, nor height and depth, nor any other created thing (Rom 8:38 ff.).

On the threshold of missions week, these are the realities of which we need most to be assured, lest our lives and hearts are anchored in the wrong world: The crowned Christ above creates His Church below; the crowned Christ above commissions His Church below; and the crowned Christ above confirms His church below.

DEAN O. WENTHE

Prof. Wenthe is currently an associate professor of Hebrew and Old Testament at Concordia Theological Seminary, Ft. Wayne, where he has served on the faculty since 1980. Prior to that he was pastor at Zion Lutheran Church, Atlantic, Iowa from 1976-80 and also assistant professor in Hebrew and Old Testament from 1971-76 at CTS when it was in Springfield, Illinois. Prof. Wenthe graduated with distinction from Concordia Senior College, Ft. Wayne, Indiana, in 1967 and from Concordia Seminary, St. Louis with an M. Div. in 1971. He also received a Master of Theology Degree from Princeton Theological Seminary in 1975 and a Master of Arts in Theology in 1985 from Notre Dame, where he is now a Ph. D. candidate in theology. Prof. Wenthe has presented numerous papers and essays and served as Associate Editor of the *Concordia Self-Study Bible.* He also served on the archeological staff of the University of Notre Dame, Capernaum, Israel in 1985 & 1986.

GOD AS COMMUNICATOR:
THE OLD TESTAMENT MODEL

Prof. Dean O. Wenthe

It is worth noting that a part of the "holy joy" which moved the early church and which Dr. Henry alluded to yesterday flowed from their love of Sacred Scripture. Our fathers in the faith were molded in their assumptions and actions by the Biblical texts which they integrated into their thinking and lives with remarkable results. Perhaps there was less noise to clutter their consciences and less media to interrupt their reflection.

Whatever the advantages or disadvantages of their setting, we are surely well served by first searching the Scriptures—and *then* developing our mission strategies.

In fact, the primitive church is a superlative model in this regard. If we could recapture, at every level of the church's life, a *delight* in Scripture, similar to that which is described by the poet in Psalm 1,

in the Torah is his delight...
and in the Torah he meditates day and
night (v. 2),

then our missionary endeavors would also be marked by a new clarity and natural energy—a greater conviction and glad confession of the Biblical truth.

It is within this framework of assumptions that we want to explore afresh the Old Testament with particular attention to the portrait it provides of *God as Communicator: the Old Testament Model.*

To address this topic I would like to characterize briefly the way in which the Old Testament is viewed in our culture and even frequently in the church.

Secondly, we will review very briefly where the scholarly community is presently located with respect to our topic.

And then, having positioned ourselves within the present context, we will explore several major contours of God's communication in the Old Testament. Due to the brevity of our time, I will distill these broad overviews into several theses for your consideration. These theses, in turn, will hopefully increase your delight in Torah—in Sacred Scripture—and spark that "holy joy" which will define the church's missionary task in that vocabulary and with that vision that only God himself could provide.

How did God communicate in the Old Testament?

Let us begin to address that question by sharing one answer that comes from outside the Old Testament, but which was offered by a community which devoutly read its pages and reflected on its meaning for their lives.

The Bavli or Babylonian Talmud records the following tale about an ancient non-Missouri synod cleric:

A. Four hundred barrels of wine turned sour on Rabbi Huna. Rabbi Judah, the brother of Rabbi Sela the Pious, and a company of rabbis came to see him. They said to him, "The master should take a good look at his deeds!"

B. He said to them, "And am I suspect in your eyes?"

C. They said to him, "And is the Holy One, blessed be he, suspect of inflicting a penalty without justice?"

D. He said to them, "Has anybody heard anything bad about me? Let him say it."

E. They said to him, "This is what we have heard: the master does not give to his hired hand his share of the vine twigs."

F. He said to them, "Does he leave me any! He steals all of them to begin with."

G. They said to him, "He does this in line with the saying, steal from the thief who has stolen from you."

H. He said to them, "I pledge that I'll give them to him."

I. Some say that the vinegar turned back into wine, and some say that the price of vinegar went up so he sold it off at the price of wine.[1]

As tempting as it is to draw from this tale a pastoral application as to what the faculty might do if Dr. Voelz's wine cellar suffered a similar fate, the obvious point of the parable is the cause/effect nature of God's communication with mankind:

Rabbi Huna's four hundred barrels of wine are now vinegar.
Therefore, the Holy One, blessed be he, has spoken!

His fellow faculty members exegete this event for Rabbi Huna: "You are guilty!"

To this day, there is a large segment of the Christian community which basically delivers a Talmudic interpretation of God's communication with humanity in the Old Testament.

The popular assumption that God's communication in the Old Testament mode felled people with mathematical precision, is perhaps fed by Hollywood's portrayal of Moses in The Ten Commandments. This model, wherein God descends on us with proportionate punishment for each misdeed, is then contrasted with the New Testament's communication of God with man in the love and mercy displayed by Christ.

This juxtaposition of God as communicator of law in the Old Testament and revealer of love in the New Testament—so accurately chronicled in John Bright's *The Authority of the Old Testament*—partially explains the propensity of even pastors to prefer New Testament rather than Old Testament texts for preaching and teaching.[2]

If most of us here, with Job, would protest this portrait of God's communication in the Old Testament, it remains our task to describe *how* we would construe God's communication.

The initial move in describing God's communication with mankind in the Old Testament must be a step backward so that the full range of texts can be taken into account. In other words, any simplistic cataloguing of prophetic formulas such as "Thus says the Lord," followed by propositions on the nature of revelation would skew the data. With Augustine, we would urge that no single category will suffice to capture the richness of God's role as communicator with mankind as described in the Old Testament.

If we are to practice and not simply parrot the *Sola Scriptura* principle, then our first move will lead us a very great distance indeed. It will lead us across millennia of time and across major cultural barriers.

To put it pointedly, we must begin our pilgrimage with a

profound awareness that the world of Abraham, Isaac, and Jacob, of Moses, of Elijah, Ezra, and, I would add, that of Jesus of Nazareth, for he came to a community that understood itself in the categories of Second Temple Jerusalem: these worlds were quite different from our cultural milieu or that religious vision which is constructed by a Jimmy Swaggart or a Robert Schuller as they paint their canvases with the sentimentality and religiosity of twentieth century America.

I seriously doubt that Abraham, Moses, Peter, and Paul would recognize that deity which emerges from some of our "best" religious communicators as the God of Israel whom they worshipped and served.

Again, our calling is to create in our missionary communication the Biblical realities, i.e., to hold before the masses not a collage of phrases that will lead to action only, but a vocabulary which will lead to the God of Israel and the Father of Jesus Christ. The actions which then follow should reflect and further hold up this missionary Biblical vision.

If we look beyond the general populace to the privileged few in academic posts, the data are equally intriguing.

First, as we glance at the terrain of current Old Testament scholarship and locate our topic vis-a-vis other descriptions, it is interesting that a vast literature has addressed the prior question of what unifying theme, or themes, can be drawn from the Old Testament, and, at the same time, encompass the whole spectrum of the canon's witness.[3]

Not a few scholars have simply despaired. For example, James Barr and others have to a great extent recommended that any search for an underlying unity in the Old Testament should be abandoned, i.e., one can only speak of the Yahwist's portrayal of God's communication, wisdom's view of God as communicator, etc.[4]

The summaries of Gerhard Hasel's *Old Testament Theology: Basic Issues of the Current Debate* and Brevard Child's *Introduction to the Old Testament as Scripture* are excellent introductions to this scholarly discussion. Not to exhaust, but to give you a sample of the proposals for a unifying theme or concept, the following are noteworthy:

1. Walter Eichrodt proposes "Covenant."[5].

2. Gerhard von Rad suggests "A history of Traditions."[6]
3. Walter Kaiser posits "The Promise" Theme.[7]
4. G. E. Wright concludes "The Mighty Acts of God" is central.[8]
5. Hasel's own multiplex approach seeks to incorporate several major emphases.[9]

We should also look at how the New Testament, the Fathers, Luther, and their pre-Enlightenment students posited the unity of the Old Testament. At each step of this investigation, it is necessary to recognize the hermeneutical environment in which we do our analysis.

These answers are prominent in recent Old Testament studies. But another perspective which is currently enjoying a revival of interest should be mentioned for completeness, namely the *Religionsgeshichte* stream of investigation, usually credited in its Old Testament application to the creativity of Herman Gunkel.[10] This approach would subsume the whole Old Testament under the inclusive category of Ancient Near Eastern religions so that any distinctiveness of Israel's Scriptures tends to be reduced to only those strands which can be demonstrably pronounced indigenous (somewhat like the criterion of dissimilarity that has been used on the sayings of Jesus).

What we have at stake in these discussions, of course, is that the answer relative to the unity of the Old Testament necessarily invites inferences about the chief trait or traits which the authors are communicating about God through these texts, or, for our topic, how God is communicating.

If we use the classical assumptions concerning the Old Testament, namely, that it is all "communication from God," and offer several motifs—not all that could be listed!—but several that should surely be in any assessment of God's role as communicator, our discussion will assume more concrete contours.

First of all—and over against other Ancient Near Eastern cosmologies such as the Enuma Elish—the Old Testament assumes that God is in relationship, i.e., he communicates with each human being by virtue of the act of creation.[11]

It is very striking that this fundamental role of the Old Testament God as communicator is questioned in a recent anthropology by Wolfhart Pannenberg. He writes:

As a historical claim about the beginnings of human history, the idea that there was an original union of humankind with God which was lost through a fall to sin is incompatible with our currently available scientific knowledge about the historical beginnings of the race. This being the case, we should renounce the artificial attempts to rescue traditional theological formulae....[12]

Thus the fundamental unity of the human race in their origin and innocence is no longer assumed. The Old Testament not only assumes it, but teaches that we are all "from Adam." Furthermore, our first parents were "innocent" and not "ashamed." Tucked into the very opening chapters of Genesis is the assumption that all mankind is *coram Deo,* before God.

Christian theology until the Enlightenment and in some quarters even thereafter has simply assumed that God was not silent even when man tries to silence him. The Flood narrative of Genesis 6-9 clearly claims to be inclusive, for God considers the possibility of eliminating the work of Genesis 2—so persistently pernicious is man's will and nature!

Two key categories in expounding this truth were linked and formed the basis of many learned Medieval tomes.

First, "the image and likeness of God" (Gen 1:26, 9:6) was the organizing principle for an anthropology that has also had a significant place for "natural law" categories.

Luther, for example, in a pessimistic moment urges the Germans at least to be good Turks and act with an awareness of the natural law.[13] He was sure that God had communicated his law to man by virtue of creation.

Everywhere one looks in the Old Testament, there is evidence that God is viewed as a communicator, not only with Israel, but with the whole human race. Genesis 11 with its human strategy of rebellion in tower building assumes a similar and inclusive framework. All of humanity is described as standing before God. Much later, in Psalm 2, God's belly laughter meets the nations who revolt against the Lord and against his Anointed, the Messiah.

How does this impact our missionary task? The Old Testament would suggest that we can target the Gospel to listeners who are "in Adam," "in the image of God," i.e., there will be an awareness of the "deus absconditus," the hidden God whose "nomos" surrounds the being of every man. We can point to this reality in the proclamation of the law, even as we prepare for the Gospel's articulation. The Old Testament not only stands over against any gnosticism which would challenge the goodness of God's creation, it also would root anthropology in the image of God and in Adam. To forfeit the role of God as Communicator in creation and human nature would have the profoundest consequences for our understanding of peoples everywhere and for our task of sharing God's Word.[14]

If we move from this fundamental understanding of God's general and inclusive communication to his more specific communication with the distinctive promise of the Gospel, our cultural assumptions will again be challenged.

His communication comes from a very strange quarter: from Israel! Not from one of the high cultures of Mesopotamia! Not from the urbane cities of Egypt!

From our perspective, and properly so in one sense, the only history that mattered in antiquity was the history of Israel.

But, from the perspective of Abraham and Moses, of Elijah and Ezra, the claims of God and His promises were heard and stated amidst what appeared an incredible incongruity.

On the one hand, God could promise Abram that the consequences of "his seed" would involve a blessing upon all nations.

On the other hand, Abram found himself not in the seat of prominence, not a broker of power in any of the great civilizations and nations, but one of countless tribal chieftains who could have passed through ancient Ebla. While Genesis 14 states that he could muster 318 trained men for territorial combat to rescue Lot and family, the text also credits God's presence with the victory.

As we've unearthed Ebla, a city with several thousand bureaucrats to monitor taxes and extensive trading, it is clear that the passing of Abram and his family would have gone unnoticed. By every human measure, Abram was not a major military or economic presence in Canaan during that period. He was simply another Bedouin prince.

No one, by human standards, would have hinged the fate of the multiplex and refined civilizations of antiquity on the blood-line of another, passing Bedouin chieftain. Yet Yahweh does precisely that in Genesis 12:3:

I will bless those who bless you, and whoever curses you I will curse; and all peoples on earth will be blessed through you.

This Messianic promise suggests our first thesis:

God's communication in the Old Testament was incarnational! Look at the Old Testament. The very texts which modern Bible classes tend to rush through or skip entirely—the genealogies—are the ones which are held up in Genesis as pivotal and key. In fact, the patriarchal narratives are largely a history of finding a suitable mate and above all having a child!

In our atomized and highly individualized culture, the punch and point of these Old Testament genealogies is easily lost, namely, that the fate of all rides on the events connected with the few.

In fact, the Old Testament claims that the destiny of all depends not even on the few, but on the *one:* the seed of the woman—Gen 3:15—the line of Seth—of Noah—of Shem—the seed of Abraham, Isaac, Jacob, of Judah, and of David. All have their end (*telos*) in Jesus of Nazareth.

Surely when Matthew, so clearly addressing his history of Jesus to a Jewish audience, begins his Gospel with the majestic line "the account of the genealogy of Jesus Christ, son of David, son of Abraham," he has said it all! The Messianic promises— tied to the specific line of blood which God specified—would bring forth that singular seed who would both represent the whole nation and redeem all of mankind.

As Luther puts it in an interesting summary of his reflection:

If Adam, Noah, and other patriarchs had lived at the time of Abraham, who received the new promise, it would have been necessary for them to believe that Christ would be of the seed of Abraham, or they would have lost God, who promised the coming of the seed.

If Abraham had lived at the time of David, it would have been necessary for him to believe that the coming of Christ would be of the lineage of David, or he would have believed in vain in the seed of a woman.

If David had lived at the time of John the Baptist, it would have been necessary for him to believe in Jesus, the seed of his descendent Mary, or he would have perished.

If John the Baptist had lived after the resurrection—no, if he had believed, in his own time, that Christ would come or had not yet come—he would have been damned.

A feature of this *incarnational communication* is that it entailed and required God's action in space and time, i.e., by his grace God sustained the blood that would issue forth in the Messianic seed.

Hence, Gen 12 through II Kings spends a great deal of time talking about the land which God would give according to his promise. This was a land admirably able to sustain this people who were indeed peculiar, chosen by God to be his own, chosen by him to articulate another view of the world. It was a view provided by and communicated Yahweh, the creator God.

This particularity, this specificity of the Old Testament's portrait of God as communicator should cause us to pause. It is precisely parallel to the scandal of the cross!

That God should choose to communicate the good news through such means still strikes our reason as an inefficient and even inappropriate way for the God of all power to express himself.

Indeed, when we put Israel under a magnifying glass, the offense is all the greater. From its inception, Israel's majority inclined toward golden calves of one sort or another. Even as a whole generation was to die in the wilderness, so the dark generations of the Judges period attest the flightiness of Israel's faith. The fact that *good* King Josiah was unfamiliar with the Pentateuch, after its recovery and reading in 622, attests to the completeness of Judah's apostasy.

Israel, which was to be an incarnational light to the nations, too often flickered so severely that great men of God like Elijah and Jeremiah wondered whether there were any who believed in Yahweh's promise. Yet, the promise was there! The seed of Abraham would decide the outcome of all human history!

A second thesis that I would submit for your consideration is that *God's communication in the Old Testament was sacramental!*

Again, we must shed our cultural prejudices which assume that all "true religion" is private and "spiritual," i.e., a matter exclusively between God and my soul. The altars of the patriarchs, the elaborate provisions for the tabernacle in Exodus, the extensive stipulations for sacrifices, the ordering of priests and Levites—all of these were God's way of concretely communicating theological truths to Israel. All one need do is consult a work on ancient Israel like Roland de Vaux's to see how central sacrifice and sanctuary were to God's plan for Israel.[16]

Or, to quote an exegete from the orthodox period of Lutheranism (1557), John Chytraeus, in his *Commentary on Leviticus,* writes:

> Under the topic of an Anatomy of Christ's Sacrifice an analog of Christ's propitiatory sacrifice can also be discerned in all its types and presentations which God set forth in such a manifold way in the Old Testament.

> He did this in order that there might continually be signs, reminders, and occasions for teaching the people about the future sacrifice of God's son, which alone expiates and takes away the sin of the world.

> Such shadows and representations were Abel's lamb, the sacrifice of Isaac, the Passover lamb, the brass serpent lifted up in the wilderness, and, finally, all the burnt offerings and sacrifices—the sin offering, the trespass offering, and others which the Levitical priests daily offered to God.[17]

If we add to these the central significance of the Temple, with the divine specifications for its construction, not to mention the key role of the arc of the covenant, and focus on the worship life of Israel, we are in the presence of a God who communicates through what we might call sacraments or sacramentals.

Read the Psalms of Ascent, or, listen to the lament of God's people in Psalm 137 as they remember Zion:

> By the waters of Babylon, there we sat down and wept
> When we remembered Zion.
> On the willows there, we hung up our lyres,

For there our captors required of us songs, and our
tormentors mirth, saying, "Sing us one of the songs of
Zion!"
How shall we sing the Lord's song in a foreign land?
If I forget you, O Jerusalem, let my right hand wither!
Let my tongue cleave to the roof of my mouth,
If I do not remember you,
If I do not set Jerusalem above my highest joy!

I believe it is safe to say that few Lutherans have that sort of
sentiment toward their sanctuary!

Or listen to the exuberant joy of Psalm 126:

When the Lord restored the fortunes of Zion,
We were like those who dream.
Then our mouth was filled with laughter
And our tongues with shouts of joy.

How beautifully this sentiment turns to a confession of
Yahweh before the nations!

Then they said among the nations,
"The Lord has done great things for them.
The Lord has done great things for us;
We are glad!"

This is precisely the conceptuality which shaped the early
church's liturgy. The sacraments were great things done by God
and continuous with his mighty deeds in Israel.

As Cardinal Danielou has written:

For the fact is that the life of ancient Christianity was
centered around worship. And worship was not considered
to be a collection of rites meant to sanctify secular life.

The sacraments were thought of as the essential events of
Christian existence and of existence itself, *as being* a
prolongation of the great works of God in the Old
Testament and the new.[18]

Worship, the response of God's people to God's gracious acts,
was a public witness which recommends another view of
reality.

It's not sufficient for the Old Testament, nor for Lutherans who
have rejected the impulses of the radical Reformation, to reduce
God's communication exclusively to the head or to the heart or to
some disembodied spirituality. God is truly present in this

Incarnation and in the Sacraments. The Old Testament provided that same conceptuality to understand God As Communication with mankind.

And here we come full circle, for the final thesis I would offer is that *God's communication in the Old Testament—just opposite the portrayal of our introductory parable—is an expression of God's grace.*

The God of the Old Testament is not disposed to change your wine to vinegar nor your life to death!

His communication is distinguished by *grace.* This grace is most sharply focussed in the gracious promise of the woman's seed—the Messiah.

The way in which God used the weak and obscure, the faltering and faithless people of Israel, precisely parallels the genealogy of Matthew wherein Jesus comes from the disappointing line of a woman with no inherent power.

Indeed, Paul—that great lover of the Old Testament—beheld in his own service the same *sola gratia* orientation of God.

Paul, whom opponents characterized as a poor speaker and of weak presence (2 Cor. 10), was following in the footsteps of Jesus, whom men similarly mistook for Jeremiah or one of the prophets. In the Old Testament, God the communicator comes on the low road of the Gospel promise and the sacraments.

And this places us, from the human perspective, in a paradox, a divinely and Scripturally ordered paradox, namely "cur alii...non alii?" Why some and not others?

There is a particularism about the promise. Isaiah's majestic prophecy of the great shoot which will come forth from the stump of Jesse locates the eschatalogical deliverance in the hiddenness of Israel's foreseen demise and concludes with:

In that day the root of Jesse shall stand

as an ensign to the peoples;

him shall the nations seek,

and his dwelling shall be glorious.

This great day is also marked

by the restoration of creation.

The wolf shall dwell with the lamb.

(Is. 9:10-11)

Thus, here and elsewhere (e.g., Is 56 & 66) God is portrayed

as holding up the particular for the benefit and/or the judgment of
the universe.

What all of this shows, I would suggest, is that the Old
Testament description of God as Communicator is another
perspective on the face of Christ: I and the Father are one, in this
sense, that our mission is to use God's means of Word and
Sacrament—that low and obscure road by which God graciously
first promises and then incarnates a Savior in the hiddenness of
the cross.

When all is said and done, the peculiar history of a minor
Palestinian clan in antiquity precisely parallels another Palestinian,
whose personal history seemed equally irrelevant for the destiny
of mankind.

But, as Paul states, God's object in using such means is nothing
else than that "no flesh might boast in his presence!"
(1 Cor. 1:29).

This Biblical realism and truth plants our mission vision on
God's soil and will spare us the empire-building and grandiose
agendas which men so easily interpret as God's will and then
behold it fall as flat as the PTL paradigm.

The low road of Word and Sacrament, the path that God
walked in his role as Communicator in the Old Testament is the
road our Lord calls us to walk in our witnessing to the
nations.

1. Cited in Jacob Neusner, *Judaism: The Classical Statement.* The Evidence of
the Bavli. (Chicago: The University of Chicago Press, 1968), p. 30.
2. John Bright, *The Authority of the Old Testament* (Nashville: Abingdon,
1967).
3. A good example is A.H.G. Gunneweg's *Understanding the Old Testament,*
ET, London and Philadelphia, 1978.
4. James Barr, *The Bible in the Modern World* (London and Philadelphia,
1973).
5. Walter Eichrodt, *The Bible in the Modern World* (London and Philadelphia:
Westminster Press, I 1961; II, 1967).
6. Gerhard von Rad, *Old Testament Theology* (ET, Edinburgh and New York,
I, 1962; II, 1965).
7. Walter C. Kaiser, *Toward an Old Testament Theology* (Grand Rapids:
Zondervan, 1978).
8. G.E. Wright, *God Who Acts,* Studies in Biblical Theology (London and
Naperville, 1952).

9. G.F. Hasel, *Old Testament Theology. Basic Issues in the Current Debate* (Grand Rapids: Wm. B. Eerdmans, 1975).

10. H. Gunkel, "Ziele und Methoden der Erklarung des Alten Testaments," *Reden und Aufsatze* (Gottingen: Templemann 1913) pp. 11-19.

11. James Pritchard, *Ancient Near Eastern Texts* (Princeton: Princeton University Press, 1969).

12. Wolfhart Pannenberg, *Anthropology in Theological Perspective* (Philadelphia: The Westminster Press, 1986, p. 57).

13. Paul Althaus, *The Ethics of Martin Luther* (ET Philadelphia: Fortress Press, 1972, p. 33 ftn 46).

14. Edward A. Malloy, "The Problem of Methodology in Contemporary Roman Catholic Ethics," *St. Luke's Journal of Theology* (1978), Vol. xxii, No. 1, pp. 20-42.

15. Theses 12-15, *The Licentiate Examination of Heinrich Schmedenstele, 1542. WA* #39, 188.7. Cited in Heinrich Bornkamm, *Luther and the Old Testament* (Philadelphia: Fortress Press, 1969) p. 110.

16. Roland de Vaux, *Ancient Israel: Its Life and Institutions,* (New York: McGraw-Hill Book Company, 1961).

17. John Chytraeus, *De Sacrificiis,* tr. John Warwick Montgomery (St. Louis: Concordia Publishing House, 1962), p. 86.

18. Cardinal Jean Danielou, *The Bible and the Liturgy* (South Bend: University of Notre Dame Press), p. 17.

JAMES W. VOELZ, Ph. D.

Dr. Voelz has served on the faculty of Concordia Theological Seminary, Ft. Wayne, since 1976. He is currently associate professor in the Department of Exegetical Theology. He received a B. A. from Concordia Senior College, Ft. Wayne, in 1967, an M. Div. from Concordia Seminary, St. Louis in 1971, and a Ph. D. from Cambridge University, England in 1978. He has also studied at the University of Basel and Oxford University, and in 1983 he was accepted into membership in the Society of New Testament Studies. He is the author of *Fundamental Greek Grammar,* published by Concordia Publishing House, and of numerous other publications. He coaches indoor and outdoor soccer at the Seminary and has served as Pastoral Assistant at Zion Lutheran Church, Ft. Wayne since 1983. He lives in Ft. Wayne with his wife Judy and son Jonathan.

GOD AS COMMUNICATOR:
THE NEW TESTAMENT MODEL

James W. Voelz, Ph. D.

I. Introduction:
God's activity on our behalf and his communication to us

Communication is important. It is a truism of modern life. Every Sunday we see advertisements for GTE with Dick Enberg, talking about the necessity and importance of communication in modern NFL football, and it is well known to all that a key—if not *the* key—to a successful marriage is good wholesome communication. But this is never the whole story. It is especially not the whole story in Christianity. One of my professors from seminary days used to say that all theologies have a theory of salvation (soteriology), and that all these theories of salvation are reducible to two: either Christ essentially *did* something or he essentially *revealed*—communicated—something to man. (Not that the two are mutually exclusive, but I am talking about the so-called "bottom line".) And the fact of the matter is that what is ultimately important in our Savior's mission is *not* what he *said,* so that we may follow his commands, *but* rather what he *did,* so that we may fear, love, and trust in him above all things. Nonetheless, God *did* reveal, through our Lord and through others, so many and such wonderful things, and what has been revealed is so tremendously important—and, indeed, God's communicating to us is the topic of this Congress and of this paper—so it is to this topic which we now turn: "God as Communicator: the NT Model," remembering always that God has *not only talked to us;* more importantly he has *redeemed us* lost and condemned creatures, from sin, from death, and from the power of the devil.

II. Communication Through Deeds

It may be surprising to learn that the first section of this presentation on communication begins with deeds. Some may ask, "Is this possible? Is this a logical division of the topic?" The answer is that we do communicate through deeds; as we all know, "Actions speak louder than words." Therefore, I want to begin by reminding us all that communication does take place through deeds and activities, and that such communication is powerful—more powerful, in many instances, than any utterance of words.

A. Actors

When God communicated through deeds at the time of the New Testament, who were the agents of his communication, that is to say, as he so communicated, who were the actors who performed these communicating deeds? Many people could be mentioned, but it is clear that two (two people and/or two groups) are most important.

1. Christ Jesus, God incarnate. The first is Jesus of Nazareth, our Lord and Savior, Jesus Christ. He is very God. That is to say, in him God walked the earth, and in him, to quote St. Paul, "dwelt the fullness of the Godhead bodily" (Col 2:9). This means that when Jesus acted, God acted. As Jesus says to Philip, in John, Chapter 14:

> Do you not believe that I am in the Father and the Father is in me?. . . The Father remains in me and does his works (v. 10). Believe me, that I am in the Father and the Father in me, or else, believe on account of the works themselves (v. 11).

As a result, when Jesus acted, God communicated with us, for with all activity communication does take place. This is why John calls Jesus the "Word" in the first verse of the first chapter of his Gospel (John 1:1):

> In the beginning was the Word, and the Word was with God, and the Word was God.

What does it mean to call Jesus the "Word"? It may mean, and does mean, many things, but at this point we can say that it signifies that Jesus is the *perfect communication from God,* i.e., that in everything Jesus was, and in everything Jesus did, God communicated with man—indeed, that in Christ he gave the highest and most important communication to men, a revelation of himself. As John records it, again, in Jesus' conversation with Philip:

> Philip said to him, "Lord, show us the Father, and it is sufficient," (v. 8). Jesus said to him, "For such a length of time I have been with you and you have not known me, Philip? He who has seen me hasiseen the Father" (v. 9).Jesus Christ our savior is, then, the prime actor whose deeds give us a communication from God.

    2. His appointed authorities (apostles). But there are other New Testament actors as well. There are also God's appointed authorities. These are the apostles. What was an apostle? The word "apostle" does not really mean "one who is sent." Rather, it means a *fully-empowered ambassador*—one who speaks *and acts* totally for his master. We can see this concept in action in Matthew, Chapter 10:

> And summoning his twelve disciples, he gave *them authority* over evil spirits, so as to cast them out, and to heal every disease and every malady (what Jesus himself did) (v. 1). . . .
> And he said: "He who receives you receives me, and he who receives me receives him who sent me" (v. 40).

It is hard to overestimate the importance of this passage, for it reveals that, as the apostles acted, their acts were the very acts of God.

    B. Nature of the Actions

    What, then, is the *nature* of the actions and activities through which God communicated to men?

    1. Divine—supernatural elements. On the one hand, they can be characterized as having divine elements; they partook in the supernatural. As far as *our Lord* is concerned, this, of course, is clear. He did many miracles and extraordinary things, and, one might even say, it is for these that he is best known by both Christians and non-Christians alike. Matthew 11:2-5 is a good illustration here:

> John, after he had heard in prison of the deeds of Christ, sent via his disciples a message and said to him: are you the one who is coming, or should we await another? And Jesus replied and said to them: "Go tell John what you hear and see: the

blind regain their sight, the lame walk, lepers are cleansed, the deaf hear, the dead are raised, and the poor have the good news preached to them." These same deeds were done by the *apostles,* when they received power from their Lord. A few moments ago I quoted Matthew 10:1, where Jesus gave his disciples authority over all sorts of evil. That passage continues:

Go and proclaim, the Kingdom of Heaven has drawn near. Heal the sick, raise the dead, cleanse lepers, cast out demons (vv. 7-8).

Paul calls these kinds of deeds "the signs of an apostle" in 2 Cor 12:12, and as an apostle, he was able to do them, too.

2. Human—natural elements. On the other hand, there are human elements, natural elements, in the activities of God's actors, as well. In our Lord we see all that belongs to humanity—he became tired (John 4:6), he became thirsty (John 19:28), he became angry (Mark 1:41). He looked and acted like a man. (Is there a problem in "Away in a Manger," verse 2: "the little Lord Jesus no crying he makes"?) The same can be said of apostles. In them one can see all the humanity exhibited in our Lord, and this is very natural, for they were human beings first of all. We see boldness in Peter, timidity in Andrew, cooperation in Philip, feistiness in Paul (not to mention fear [Acts 1] and lack of understanding [Gal. 1]). They, too, looked and acted just like men.

Yes, in the actions of Jesus and his apostles, we see participation in all that is human and in all that is divine.

C. Interpretation of. . .

How do we now *interpret* the actions by which God communicates to men? The actions I have just described can and should be interpreted— and as Christians that is our task. Let me move to this next section by saying, however, that these actions—these God-communicating actions—had an *effect;* they *worked salvation:* they brought health, healing, and wholeness to those whom they touched (they were not simply demos!), and we must never minimize this fact (cf. introduction).

. . . events can and must be "read," even as words are read

How are actions communication? As I said at the beginning

of this section, actions do communicate; by themselves they "speak" (louder than words). We might say that they—activities and actions—*have significance.* They signify something beyond themselves. We know this in everyday life, and we act accordingly. If a young teenage boy begins to hang around and associate with girls, we know what that means. If a church member ceases to attend worship and the Sacrament of the Altar regularly, it "tells" us about his spiritual life. If a husband works late every night and takes every opportunity to stay away from home, a wife can "read" that activity like a book. You can multiply examples. Just so, we must "read" the activities in Scripture, as we read activities in life.

But *how* do we read people's acts? What is our *basis* for interpretation? In everyday life, it is our *experience of life* which is our guide. We know life, so we can interpret it. And with the Bible? What is our guide in its interpretation? For things that pertain to human nature, again, life is our guide. But for the *divine* aspect of activities it depicts, for these our life is *not* our guide. Rather, here we need a knowledge of God and of his promises to give us a context for interpretation. Where do we find such knowledge to be our aid? *Only in the holy book!* Only in the Scriptures. We must use the Scriptures themselves to interpret the deeds of our Lord and of his apostles, for only here do we have a proper background against which to understand these activities and acts. Consider again Matthew 11:2-5. How are the acts of these verses to be understood? (Indeed, how was John the Baptist supposed to "read" these acts— since our Lord did not explain them?) By reading the Old Testament—the context, the experiential basis, so to speak, for interpreting these acts! In this particular instance, this means by reading Isaiah 35:4-6a:

> Say to them that are of a fearful heart, "Be strong, fear not: behold, your God will come with vengeance, he will come with recompense to save you. Then the eyes of the blind shall be opened, and the ears of the deaf unstopped. Then shall the lame man leap like a hart, and the tongue of the dumb sing for joy."

Here we find the *precedent* for the acts of Matthew 11:2-5—here is the background for interpretation. Against this kind of "Scriptural experience" Christ's actions can be read.

And what do these actions of our Lord now mean? What is the

content of, what is the *message* of these acts? The message, I think, is clear. First of all, these acts "say" that Jesus himself is God. *God,* Isaiah said, will come with recompense; he—and he alone—will come to save. In Jesus, God is now here, that is what the healings and the resurrections show. Secondly, these acts "say" that God desires to save, that he is a loving God, that he is not a vicious God, that he has the welfare of his people in his heart. And not only that, they say that he has put that desire into effect, so that he, in Christ, has actually come to accomplish our salvation. Indeed, this is the true central message of both the Old and New Testaments alike. Thirdly, things are now different, this we can read from these acts. Isaiah describes (in his larger context) what things will be like in the age to come—in that time when God will set all things right. That time is *now,* the acts of Jesus plainly say. The age to come is *now,* in him that age is *here;* things are different *now,* we clearly read, for in him is the salvation of our God.

And what do these activities mean when they are done by the apostles of our Lord (you will remember that they were commissioned to do the same things by our Lord (Matthew 10), and they did, in fact, accomplish them)? Again, the message is plain. In their activities and deeds, God, too, was at work; God was at work in them, so that *in them*—in all that they did for him (for God)—the age to come was present and available to all.

What, then, about the human side of acts? What about those features of the activity of our Lord and of the apostles which exhibit purely human traits? As far as such activity is concerned, we are left to our own experience to interpret, as I have said, but, given our knowledge of life, the interpretation of truly human acts is not difficult at all. What does it mean that Jesus was tired, thirsty, angry, hungry. and so on? These acts "tell" us that he was truly human, that he was fully one of us. In the words of the Book of Hebrews, that he was like us in every way, except for sinning (4:15), and again, that in him we have a high priest who can truly sympathize with us (4:15). The same may be said for the apostles of our Lord. Because of who they were and because of the way they acted, we are now "told" that to be a Christian does not mean losing one's personality, and we are "told" that God can and does use all kinds of people for his work. God uses humans not machines when he communicates on earth.

Yes, actions can speak louder than words, and the activities of our Lord and of his chosen ambassadors can, and should, speak volumes to us now.

III. Communication through Words

Normally, when we think of communication, we think of verbal communication; we think of communication through words. And how true this really is. Actually, the use of complex and developed language systems is probably that which is most characteristic of humanity as such, distinguishing us from the animals, and setting us apart as the very crown of the entire creation of God. And it is to such linguistic usage which we now turn. As with the section concerning deeds, we will consider, first, the performers or speakers (cf. actors), then the nature of the discourse (cf. actions), and finally the interpretation of the discourse as part of God's communication to man.

A. Speakers

Who are the speakers for God in the New Testament revelation?

1. Christ Jesus, God incarnate. Again, number one is Christ, he who is God incarnate. Consider again John 1:1. Our Lord, these words assert, is our very God. He is the "Word"—the perfect communication of our God. But that is true not only of deeds, as I said before. It is also true of words. Indeed, one could argue that it is *especially* true of words, for with words one knows in depth what a man truly thinks, hopes, and believes. In the words of our Lord in the twelfth chapter of John:

I do not speak of myself, but the Father who sent me has himself commanded what I shall speak and say" (v. 49).

So, in Jesus God not only acted; in him he also spoke.

2. His appointed authorities (apostles). Secondly, God spoke through his apostles, the empowered ambassadors of Christ. They were *selected* to speak for him. In Matthew Chapter 10, we saw that Jesus gave them power, not only power to heal, but also power to proclaim: "The Kingdom of Heaven has drawn near" (v. 7). These men were also *given the words,* the very words of God. St. Paul says, I Cor 2:13:

We speak, not in words taught by human wisdom, but with words taught by the spirit.

These were the men who *were reminded* by the Holy Spirit of what had transpired in the ministry of our Lord (John 14:26), and these were the men *to whom God and his works and his words were graciously revealed,* now that the new age had come (Eph 3:1-5). Indeed, these men could be called "possessed by God," for St. Paul can actually exclaim, as he chides the Christians in Corinth:

You seek proof of Christ who is speaking in me" (II Cor 13:3).

These men spoke for Christ as the very oracles of God.

B. Nature of discourse

What, then, is the nature of the discourse comprising God's communication through words?

1. Divine—supernatural elements. Let us take the divine or supernatural elements first of all. As far as the ministry of Jesus is concerned, the words he spoke were the *very words of God* himself. The recently cited quotation from John 12:49 is proof of this, as are Jesus' own words in John 14:10:

The utterances which I speak to you I do not say of myself.

The same is also true of the apostles, as we have seen—for God gave them the words to speak; even more, God himself could be said to speak inside of them (II Cor 13:3). Actually, the divine aspect of communication relates little to the nature of the discourse of God as such, for unlike many other religions, God—either directly in Christ or through his agents, the apostles—did not do anything particularly divine linguistically, either by using exalted speech, a special speech, gibberish, or other such unusual phenomenon. The divine aspect of God's discourse relates mainly to content (cf. below) and to its effects, i.e., that it is a creative and forgiving word—creative in that it healed and forgiving in that by it, sins were actually forgiven. Yet, the discourse of Christ and the apostles in every respect was a discourse fully divine.

2. Human—natural elements. And regarding human or so-called natural elements? What can we say about these? The nature of God's discourse is fully human, whether through Jesus Christ or through the apostolic band. By all, specific, known languages were used. And the characteristics of these languages were employed, so that various literary and rhetorical devices are in evidence throughout. This has led to the formulation of Voelz's rule number one for Scriptural interpretation, namely: **the Scriptures, while**

always more than simply literature—they are the inspired and
inerrant word of God—are never less than that. While always the
words of God, they are also very fully the words of human
beings.

C. Interpretation of discourse

How, then, is God's verbal communication through Jesus Christ
and his appointed spokesmen to be understood? Here the problem is
more straightforward than in our previous major section (cf. deeds),
where it may not have been clear from the start, either *that* one
should or *how* one should interpret acts as communications at all. At
least now we are dealing with words. Just how does one interpret
words? Again, by being familiar with life and with the experience life
affords. That is to say, to interpret verbal messages in the Word of
God, we must know about other verbal communications outside that
Word of God—and this encompasses the human element in God's
verbal discourse with man. But what about the divine aspect of such
verbal communication—that element which relates chiefly to
content, not to linguistic factors as such? Here what method should
be used? I would suggest that two principles be followed: First, let
God himself interpret, insofar as he has done ("Scripture interprets
Scripture"). Secondly, *listen* to the word of God, be a hearer, not a
critic. (There is a difference between these two!) George Steiner has
put it well:

> The critic keeps his distance. . . . The reader attempts to
> negate the space between the text and himself. . . . The critic is
> judge and master of the text. . . . The reader is servant to the
> text.[1]

Let us now turn to the matter of interpretation of the divine
and human elements in the verbal communication of God
(though we will draw no distinction between Jesus Christ and
the apostles in the analysis we make).

1. Divine elements—content. The Word of God does
three things—*it interprets the acts of God; it reveals the
nature of God; and it discloses the will of God.* What is the
content of this interpretation/revelation/disclosure, as we
have it in the written word? The content is that God was in
Christ, reconciling the world to himself—the Gospel of our
God. This could be discussed for many days. Here, let me say
simply this, that according to the Scriptures, this is the *true*

revelation of our God. Another way to put it is that the Gospel tells us of God's *proper work.* Thus, God is *not really* something else. God is not really something we don't know. **God is really the Gospel God.** And there is no greater comfort than this—in times of doubt, in the sickroom, at the deathbed—throughout the Christian life. But what about passages which seem to contradict this fact? E.g., passages which tell of God's law and of God's wrath. These also stand on the basis of Scripture, and they cannot simply be set aside. Here we must follow a good principle of Scriptural interpretation which says: clear passages must never be allowed to cancel one another out but must be accepted despite the rebellion of reason at the difficulty of it all. The Gospel dare never be compromised—the Good News of God's free salvation must always reign supreme.

    2. Human elements—expression. What then about the *human elements* of God's verbal communication? Here time allows only two items to be considered, each of which is characteristic of human language whether inside the Bible or out.

    a. Modes of conveying meaning (deep and surface structure). Any interpreter must recognize and deal with the *ambiguity* which arises any time meaning is conveyed through words. This is not to say that God is not able to speak clearly. Rather, it is to recognize that all language is shorthand, and that the compressed expressions which are part of any language lead to difficulty in interpretation. A good example is the expression in English "love of God". Does this mean our love for God, i.e., that we love God, or does it signify God's love for us, i.e., that he loves us? Consider II Cor 5:14 in this regard: "The love of Christ constrains us." Does Paul here mean that we are forced to act by the love Christ has for us, or is he trying to say that we are controlled by the love we have for Christ? Either can be argued, though probably only one is actually correct. The reader must recognize that the surface structure in any language may—and very often does—conceal a number of deep structures (i.e., what is really being said), and these deep structures are the real object of investigation for interpretation.

    b. Ways of conveying thought, conception of reality (models) Any interpreter must also recognize the nature of and the importance of *figurative language* in communication. Figurative language is important, not because it is decorative or beautiful. Rather, figurative language is important because it is necessary—because it is the only way we can understand things which are unknown to us. To this end, our Lord and his apostles often used analogies. More accurately, they often used models drawn from life and spoke metaphorically on the basis of these models to reveal deep theological truths of God. An excellent example is our relationship to God. How is that relationship to be understood? There are at least 13 models—13 examples from life—which are in common NT use. These models depict for us some aspect of our relationship to God—and they are all necessary, because that relationship is so full and so complex that no one model will do. Here following are the 13 models, along with brief comments describing the aspect of our relationship to God which each model helps make clear:

1. Shepherd/sheep—God is responsible/we are helpless and needy.

2. Vine/branches—God is the source of sustenance/we need connection to him for life.

3. Bridegroom/bride—God loved us and sacrificed himself for us/we respond in obedience and love.

4. King/subjects—God has benevolent control/we are his humble people.

5. Last Adam/new creation—New life is in Christ/we participate in new life now.

6. Head/members (body)—Christ controls his church/all members are equal and necessary for the whole.

7. Elder brother/sons of the father—There is present possession of promised blessings.

8. Possessor of all/heirs—Greater gifts are yet in store.

9. Cornerstone/living stones—Christ is the key to the church/we are the dwelling place of the spirit.

10. High priest/kingdom of priests—the Old Testament covenant is continued in Christ and his church.

11. Rescuer/rescued—God is our savior/we now have freedom in him.

12. Revealer/enlightened—Christ is the source of all knowledge/we now know the truth.

13. Sacrifice/acquitted—God himself is the solution to sin/we
are not under judgment.

Are all of these models true? Yes. Are all of the models
necessary? Yes. For God in his grace and mercy has saved us, and
he has described for us our salvation, using tools—using images
which *we* can understand. That is to say, he has communicated with
us and has described heavenly things on the basis of earthly things
for us, though such description can only in each instance be partial
and incomplete. The interpreter will recognize these models for
what they are. He will use each of them as each is necessary. And he
will marvel at the complexity of our salvation, which can be
understood, not as a simple, one-surface mirror, but, rather, as a
multifaceted diamond, which shines differently at every turn.

God's verbal communication, then, is both wonderful and
complex indeed!

IV. Conclusion—Lessons for God's people

Much could be said regarding lessons of what we have said for
each and every one of us. We should take God's revelation in Christ
seriously, and we should listen to rather than judge the Word. In
addition, relating to human factors in communication, we must learn
to value semantics—the science of meaning—for as we interpret the
Holy Scriptures, we interpret the acts of both God and men, and we
interpret words, spoken by our Lord and by his apostles, as well as
those written by these same men.

I would like to conclude, however, by moving in a different
direction. And that is simply to say that *we, too,* communicate
through word and deed—or, more accurately, *God communicates
through us, too,* through our words and through our deeds. *Our very
lives* are a testimony of and to our God. Jesus said in Matthew,
Chapter 5:

"You are the light of the world" (v. 14). "Let your light so
shine before men that they may see your good works and
glorify your Father, who is in heaven" (v. 16).

And Peter said:

"Keep your conduct noble among the Gentiles, in order that
when they revile you as evildoers, they may see your good
works and glorify God on the day of visitation"
(I Peter 2:12).

Our words, too, witness to and for our God. Indeed, it is basically by the word that the kingdom of God is spread. Actions may be misread. Actions may not be understood. But a clear word is never mistaken—though a clear word may be rejected and it may be disbelieved. Yes, God communicates through us, his twentieth century children under his cross. He sends messages through us. Not in the same trans-temporal, authoritative way in which he communicated through Christ and through the apostles, his fully-empowered ambassadors. But God still works through means—not immediately—and that means through the Holy Ministry and through the sons and daughters of the king.

[1] George Steiner "Critic/Reader,;; *New Literary History* 10 (1979), 443, 449.

DAVID J. HESSELGRAVE, Ph.D.

Dr. Hesselgrave is Professor of Mission at Trinity Evangelical Divinity School in Deerfield, Illinois, where he has served on the faculty since 1965. He received a diploma in theology from Trinity in 1944, a B. A. from the University of Minnesota in 1955, where he also earned an M. A. in 1956 and a Ph. D. in Rhetoric and Public Address in 1965. He has served as pastor in Radisson, Wisconsin and St. Paul, Minnesota. He was an Evangelical Free Church missionary in Japan for twelve years and has also taught in Hong Kong and Manila. He has lectured and conducted seminars in over forty countries. Dr. Hesselgrave has written numerous articles and books, including *Communicating Christ Cross-culturally* and *Counseling Cross-Culturally*. He and his wife Selma live in Libertyville, Illinois. They are the parents of three children, two sons and a daughter.

BRIDGING CULTURES —
THEIRS AND OURS

David J. Hesselgrave, Ph. D.

Babel—a common and an uncommon view. Would it be an exaggeration to say that hardly anyone thinks of Babel in a positive way? In spite of the fact that the Hebrew means "the gate of God," connotationally Babel is negative—it speaks of judgment and confusion.

But, though seldom explicated, even divine judgment has its flipside. This was certainly true of Babel. For according to the divine record, in the early post-diluvian period "the whole earth" had the same lexicon and the same grammar. And people settled on the plain of Shinar and began to construct a central tower that would have had the effect of preventing precisely what the Creator had commanded when he said, "Be fruitful and multiply, and fill the earth, and subdue it" (Gen 1:28).

Now if we think of this first mandate in Genesis 1 as the "Cultural Mandate," then we see that Babel was one of those events that ensured that the Cultural Mandate would be carried out. Though Babel did not give rise to *culture* per se, it occasioned a dispersion of the families of mankind and therefore resulted in a diversity of *cultures*. And, given the purpose of those early peoples to centralize and build a name for themselves rather than filling and subduing the earth, it therefore had a very positive result.

Culture—defined, described, and evaluated. It is common knowledge that our word culture comes from the Latin *cultura* meaning "to till, or to cultivate." We speak of "cultivating good habits" and of a "cultured person." But anthropologists and communicologists—and will you excuse that word, because we don't really have a good word for my breed in English?—use the word in a different sense. Though they have great difficulty in agreeing on a precise definition (one text includes close to two hundred and says there are still others), they essentially agree that culture is that secondary environment that mankind imposes upon his primary, natural environment; that it is man-made, learned, and changing; and that it includes physical artifacts, sociological arrangements, and ideological frameworks.

There is no doubt that when we speak of someone as a "cultured person," we are making a positive appraisal. But what about the word in its anthropological sense—a sense that relates intimately to those events at Eden and at Shinar? At that point we may hesitate. "*Our* culture" has a positive ring to it, but "*their* culture?*" We're not so sure. And, anyway, is it not the diversity of languages and cultures that poses one of the greatest obstacles to worldwide understanding, whether in politics, economics, or religion? And, even more importantly for Christians, is it not the diversity of languages and cultures that also impedes the worldwide dissemination of the Gospel of Christ and delays the fulfillment of the *Gospel Mandate* to make disciples of all the nations?

Indeed it is. But I am going to hazard the opinion that it is not the gaps between cultures but rather the reluctance of God's people to bridge those gaps that delays the fulfillment of the Great Commission. In our day, God has afforded us every opportunity to make acquaintance with culture and cultures, to bridge cultural gaps, but we have not availed ourselves of the opportunities to bridge them.

In our post-World War II era, the missions and churches of the western world and particularly America have been brought face to face with the challenges that attend cultural diversity. Self-styled "superior" cultures and races sought to impose their rule upon us and were thwarted in the attempt. But a new era dawned. Traditional religions for which western Christians had already penned obituaries experienced new life and sent their representatives to us in record numbers. Parenthetically, I might say, with contextualized messages. People of other cultures whom we previously thought would be content to stay home and produce the rubber, oil, tin, manganese and other products essential to *our* "superior" way of life became restless and refused to stay quietly at home. Church leaders—even evangelical church leaders—gathering in Asia, Latin America and Africa not only criticized our theology, but our very way of doing it!

This state of affairs is not altogether different from that which prevailed in the New Testament world of the first century. As I. Howard Marshall (following M. Hengel) has shown us, a Sovereign God had so ordered human events that, far from being a sealed-off world, ". . . *the world of the New Testament was a world in which different cultures or ways of life were in contact with one another, leading to assimilation between them as well as to sharp collision*" (italics his).[1] (I would think that this was a part of the preparation, a part of the "fullness of times.") Then Pentecost and persecution and much more conspired to force and enable those early Christians to bridge cultural gaps and, in a relatively short period of time, the early church grew into a culturally variegated community of the redeemed. Christ indeed had conquered.

Could it be that our Sovereign Lord is opening the same possibility today—and on a global scale?

The overview of a process. This brings me to my present concern. It is not, as you might have supposed, to provide a paradigm for cross-cultural communication. I have attempted that elsewhere in a work that is approximately 500 pages in length and described as encyclopedic by one reviewer—and still does little more than scratch the surface.[2] I have even less desire to attempt to titillate with anecdotes of remarkable cross-cultural breakthroughs in the communication of Christ. Rather, I would invite you to consider the possibility that since we ourselves live and labor in the midst of a remarkable interpenetration of cultures, we may quite possibly be on the threshold of the time of the fullness of "the times of the Gentiles" of which our Lord speaks in Luke 21:24. With Donald Bloesch I believe that we must obey the Spirit who would lead us into fuller Christian obedience in our day, or we too risk the motivational fires of persecution.[3]

With that in mind, I want to overview a process by which we in missions have been brought to a new understanding of what is involved in obeying the Gospel Mandate and then invite all of you—laymen in the pew and clergy in the pulpits, missionaries in the field and educators in our schools—to join us in what may be the final effort to present Christ in an understandable and compelling way to the nations.

How Culture-Sensitive Missionary Communication
Is Carried out—
Progression in Methodology

Now if we want to know how we are to accomplish this bridging of cultures in the interest of the Gospel, one way to proceed is to give attention to the unfolding missionary process through the modern era.

The search for new tools. Paul Hiebert writes that, "Roughly from 1800 to 1950 most Protestant missionaries in India, and later in Africa, rejected the beliefs and practices of the people they served as pagan'."[4] He quotes the African John Pobee as follows:

> . . . to the present time all the historical churches by and large implemented the doctrine of the *tabula rasa,* i.e., the missionary doctrine that there is nothing in the non-Christian culture on which the missionary can build and, therefore, every aspect of the traditional non-Christian culture had to be destroyed before Christianity could be built up.[5]

This reckons without certain important data. I believe that even in the early nineteenth century, Carey, Marshman, and Ward, working in India, were deeply engaged in a study of Indian culture and customs, languages and religious writings, so much so that when this was discovered back in England, they received letters asking them whether they had been sent to convert the heathen or to be converted by them. Toward the middle of that century, Anglo-American leaders Henry Venn and Rufus Anderson were devoted to defining and developing "indigenous churches." Later, German missionaries and anthropologists were engaged in mutual discussions and endeavors designed to locate and describe foreign peoples and cultures. But it is true that sensitivity to culture has been minimal throughout the first century and a half of modern missions.

The discovery of new tools. Peter Berger and Thomas

Luckman speak of three different levels of understanding of reality (anthropologists and communicologists would prefer to speak of "world-view" and I think I can use that designation without doing violence to Berger and Luckman). First, there is the man in the street who assumes that his world-view is the only legitimate one. Those who disagree are simply ignorant or evil or both. Second, there is the sociologist who recognizes a legitimacy in differing world-views and leaves it at that. Third, there is the philosopher who senses an obligation to weigh the evidence and make value judgments.[6]

For our purposes, we can reconstruct this paradigm so as to give it special relevance to the church. We can think of the assumptions of the Christian in the pew; the new breed of missionary who recognizes the importance of differing world-views and even attributes a special kind of validity to them; and the theologian (in the wide sense of the word) whose task it is to measure alternatives by the Scriptures and the creeds of the church and perhaps, too, educate her leadership. The man or woman in the pew assumes that his or her world-view is in all respects thoroughly Christian and not subject to challenge. Traditionally, missionaries and especially theologians have evidenced a more sophisticated but obvious monoculturalism as they have gone about their respective tasks.

Belatedly, in this past generation of cross-cultural research and intercultural collision, something significant has happened in the church and its missions. It is beginning—just beginning—to filter down to the churches, to the person in the pew, and especially up to our theologians in the schools. New tools have been discovered—tools that are extremely important, not only for missionizing but ultimately for theologizing as well. From anthropology we borrow such cognitive tools as world-view, value systems, functionalism, the guilt-shame distinction, innovation and the dynamics of change. From linguistics we borrow linguistic analysis, form/meaning distinctions, dynamic equivalence, and surface and deep structures of language. From communication theory we take ideas relating to source and receptor, encoding and decoding, feedback, noise, and context. No serious study of missions today overlooks conceptual and practical tools such as these. And no candidate for a cross-cultural ministry is well-counselled who proceeds to the field without them. They are as much a part of the outfit of today's well-prepared missionary as a map, compass, pith helmet and bottle of quinine were to the missionary outfits of the previous century.

The tools applied. These new tools are gradually being applied. You can witness their application in various ways but perhaps most notably recently in the shift from the older emphasis on *indigenization* to the new emphasis on *contextualization.*

When in the nineteenth century first Venn and Anderson and then a host of others spoke of the aim of missions as being the establishment of an *indigenous* church they chose an excellent descriptive term because indigenous means to be "of the soil" or "rooted in the soil." Etymologically, then, an indigenous church would be one that would not be looked upon as fundamentally foreign to the culture in which it is growing. But when our mission forebears got around to actually defining an indigenous church they almost univocally did so in terms of the so-called "three-selfs" i.e., a self-governing, self-supporting, self-propagating church. As admirable as the establishment of such churches might be, it is also true that these three criteria are obviously of Western origin and can be misleading, as numerous analysts such as Peter Beyerhaus have now pointed out.[7] One can have a church in Tokyo that is all of these things and yet so foreign to its own culture in organization, worship, hymnology, theology, and ministry as to be almost indistinguishable from its counterpart in Toledo.

Though a few analysts still prefer the word "indigeneity" because of the liberal stance of the originators of the neologism "contextualization,"[8] the latter concept is now in the ascendancy. This change is part of a revolution in missions. What has happened? Missionary personnel have visited and revisited social scientists who have been operating on Berger and Luckman's "second level" and have adopted, adapted, and applied tools borrowed from them (the tools mentioned previously plus many others). Marvin Mayers often speaks of his "social science conversion." Charles Kraft insists that anthropologists and biculturalists are better prepared to interpret Scripture than are grammarians and historians.[9] Harvie Conn calls for a trialogue among social scientists, missionaries, and theologians.[10] Donald McGavran explains the "bridges of God" in terms provided by the social sciences.[11] Mission departments are now departments of intercultural studies. And missionary communication is cross-cultural communication. Missiology and missions will never again be the same. Alan Tippett has summarized the contemporary understanding well:

> . . . The greatest methodological issue faced by the mission in our day is how to carry out the Great Commission in a multi-cultural world, with a gospel that is both truly Christian in content and culturally significant in form.[12]

The die has been cast. Much of what has been said and proposed is excessive and some of it is actually heretical, so Tippett's reference to a message that is truly Christian in content is most appropriate. *But for good or for ill, we have entered the contextualization era.* The communicological concept of context has been widened to include culture. As cultures come more and more into contact and collision, and as a post-Christian worldview becomes increasingly prominent among Western peoples, more and more Christian communication will be seen for what it is rapidly becoming—cross-cultural and, hopefully, more culturally sensitive.

How Culture-Sensitive Missionary Communication Relates to the Great Commission—the Welcome Consequences

What happens when Christian communication becomes *truly* missionary? When it *actually* becomes culture-sensitive? When it is rightly contextualized? What happens is that the *Gospel* mandate comes closer and closer to fulfillment. (The bottom line in those definitions of "unevangelized" and "unreached" now has become "People who have had an understandable hearing of the Gospel.") But there are other gloriously positive outcomes that are not so obvious. Allow me to underscore several of these as they relate to those who are sent on cross-cultural missions themselves; to their converted respondents in other cultures; and to the theologians and academicians in the sending churches. This can best be done by resorting to specific examples.

Change in the missionary source. There is a classic little book, out of print, by H. R. Weber, with whom most missiologists at least will be familiar. In that book, *The Communication of the Gospel to Illiterates*,[13] he relates to us a beautiful story of his experience in Indonesia in Luwuk-Banggai, way in the hinterlands.

The background is this: in 1912 Muslim traders tried to convert some of its 100,000 scattered inhabitants to Islam. And as a result, the Dutch government suddenly became very missionary, and so they sent a Reformed state church minister to the area, and over a few years he travelled around and he baptized thousands of the local people. He didn't have time for instruction or follow-up and so on. Now converts, Weber says, were of three types. Some of them were sincere. Some of them felt that they had to adopt the religion of the rulers. And some became Christians in order to remain pagan. The explanation of that is that if they became Muslims they would not be allowed to keep the pigs and the dogs that were so important to their animistic sacrifices. If they became Christians, however, they could continue their pagan practices. We should understand that: we have quite a few Christians prominent in our culture who become Christian in order to remain pagan.

In 1952, Weber, an experienced missionary, was asked to go to Luwuk-Banggai and instruct the some 30,000 untutored and scattered Christians in the basics of the Bible. These were Christians in congregations, but they didn't have the word of God, and they were largely illiterate. Weber was given no money and no helpers. This was to be a Dutch treat. He went to Luwuk-Banggai and divided the area into seven districts, and he decided to hold short Bible courses in each district. He chose a team of district evangelists and ministers and invited them to come away for five days to a number of central locations. They had to pay for this in money and in kind, and that's not at all a bad idea necessarily. These students were to learn and then to share, to catechize those who were in the churches. Now the format was very simple, but profound. I can just give it to you by way of outline. Using an ingenious, contextualized method of instruction, Weber instructed these leaders in Biblical theology and Christian living. He led them along a "travel route" through the Bible from creation, to the fall, to the covenants with Israel, to the coming of

Christ and the Holy Spirit, to the formation of the Church and on
to the Revelation, with its new heavens and new earth. On the
four succeeding days, he highlighted Genesis 3, Exodus 19, then
Luke 2, and finally, Acts 1. Now each day began with worship,
the reading of the Scripture passages, prayer for guidance, then
they studied the passage in small groups, making sure that it was
linked with preceding studies, then they reported their findings,
and so on. Afternoons, they discussed community life, the
meaning of baptism, communion, evangelism, and so on. And in
the evenings, they discussed topics like "Christians in a tribal
community," "Christians in Modern Islam," "Christians in the
world," and so on.

The last evening, they emphasized the witnessing theme of
Acts 1 which then was related to these other events, so that they
had a panorama of the Scriptures. As a result of this format, many
Christians in Indonesia knew their Bible better than Christians in
North America. The last evening, they invited the whole village
where they were meeting together; they recreated the Temple in
Jerusalem and then recited Psalms 24 and 100 and then they
mimed various parables and they would ask the people to tell
them the meaning of these. After that, they would explain what
the Biblical meaning was. Then they had hymns and tea-time and
finally they had a message emphasizing Genesis 1 and
Revelation 21, with its recreated world of peace and righteousness,
and the significance of Christ's coming.

As a result of these experiences, Weber made a number of
dramatic discoveries relating to effective cross-cultural cate-
chizing—discoveries that are now being corroborated in contextualization studies. But Weber insists that he also made a
dramatic discovery concerning himself.

He said he kept hearing about tremendous Christians back in
the churches who wanted to attend his studies but could not do so
because they were *buta huruf* ("blind with regard to letters" or
illiterate). Realizing that the great majority of natives were in this
category, he made it a point to converse with them as he moved
from place to place. He discovered that though they spoke the
same language, he could barely communicate with them at all.
When he asked the meaning of a word, they would not respond
with a synonym or an abstract transcription. They would use

words to "paint a picture" that gave the exact meaning. When describing a person, they would not talk about his character but rather would tell a few experiences that pointed the kind of person he or she was. Weber began to look upon them as artists. He began to see himself as a "stunted intellectual" with but one method of communication—communication through pallid, abstract ideas. As a consequence, he became a pupil in order to learn how to communicate picturesquely and dramatically rather than intellectually and verbally. And then he tried out his discovery in one village. He assembled the whole village and asked the heathen priest to tell the story of creation as he knew it and then Weber would tell the story of creation as it is in the Scriptures. He used simple drawings on a blackboard. As a result, Weber says, he became instructed. He became the pupil. In order to teach he had to learn. And he draws some conclusions. It's a mistake to treat these people—tribalists, illiterates, semiliterates—as children merely to tell them Bible stories. And it's a mistake certainly just to preach abstract sermons. All has to be set in redemptive history, creation, eschatology, Christ the center, the history of Israel, the Church, the mission. He says that the tribalist is better equipped to understand this than the Western intellectual. And then he says all of this has to be set in contrast to the mythological framework, so that a Christian faith revolutionizes all patterns of thought.

Secondly, he says it's fundamentally wrong to translate only the New Testament or New Testament portions. It's wrong to treat only New Testament stories. Jesus the Messiah must not be de- Judaized to the extent that he is de-historicized. All this tends to put Christianity in the framework of the mythological.

Thirdly, once the mythological framework has been shattered, the classification and integrating character of what we have wrongly called "primitive thinking" should be seen as a great gift. The tribalist is able to cope with any event because he can incorporate any event into his traditional myth. The Christian can only cope because he knows the beginning, the end, the center of history. I would volunteer that Weber's discoveries, both the concepts and the tools, if utilized in our contemporary churches in the Western world, would revolutionize what we are doing and would revolutionize the understanding of our Christians and certainly make a tremendous difference when it comes to sharing the Gospel and communicating Christ to those of other world-views. That's what can happen to a missionary in this new era of which we are a part.

Weber's appreciation for the way in which God communicated his will in history and the Bible grew by leaps and bounds. And his changed communication practices resulted in profound discoveries concerning people in nonliterate cultures.

As we put forth a concerted effort to bridge cultural gaps and meaningfully communicate Scripture truth to people of other cultures, we ourselves are instructed and we ourselves change in dramatic and wholesome ways.

Change in converts in other cultures. One of the major criticisms of missionaries is that they tend to take not only their Christianity but also their Western culture to people of other cultures. So complete is this transference of "Christianity plus culture" that foreign nationals are sometimes identified as the "Dwight Moody" or the "Billy Graham" of such and such a country. Or some Western-trained and accomplished teacher becomes famous because he has mastered Barthian or some other Western theology. Now all of this has a nice ring to it until we become culture-sensitive and contextualization-conscious.

Let me illustrate. A young man with whom we became familiar in Japan had never had anything but an "A" in his educational experience and he has never had anything since, though he has now gone right through to his doctor's degree. He came to Trinity and majored in evangelism and homiletics. He wrote at the end of his sojourn a thesis for Dr. Lloyd Perry in which he gave a carefully considered overview of most of the significant evangelists of North America, going back to Finney and right on through to Billy Graham.[14] After discovering and delineating some twenty-three common characteristics, he was about to conclude that they should be incorporated in Japanese preaching. At that point his studies took an interesting turn.

Dr. Perry suggested that before he write the final chapter it might be well for him to take a course in cross-cultural communication. This seemed rather unnecessary inasmuch as Ezioh Maeda would be returning to people of his own culture. But the course proved to be revolutionary. Gradually he began to see that, as far as his Christian experience was concerned, he had been educated out of his own culture. He realized that he had heard the Gospel from a missionary; he had been trained by missionaries and Japanese theologians who themselves had been trained in the West; and almost all of his seminary textbooks had been written by Western authors. As a result he, though Japanese, had preached largely western sermons to his Japanese audiences. And as another result he had come within a hairbreadth of concluding his thesis prematurely.

After studying cross-cultural communication, Maeda added a final chapter to his thesis. In it he overviewed Japanese culture and communication. Then he wrote:

What the writer is concerned about is [a $64 question]. "How do these cultural characteristics in Japan affect the qualities of good evangelistic preaching in the United States of America?"

Japanese culture was studied with this in mind. The writer could not give easy, ready-made solutions to this problem of the relationship between paganish (sic) culture and preaching the Gospel, but at least may suggest a possible direction for solutions.

From that point, Maeda went on to re-examine the twenty-three qualities of effective preaching and in the majority of instances indicated that this characteristic should be disregarded or modified in the Japanese context! Maeda analyzed the twenty-three characteristics from a culture-sensitive point of view. In Japan, he concluded, if one wants to preach effective evangelistic sermons, he or she must probably disregard or at least change almost every one of these characteristics. They do not fit the Japanese culture. He had been in the church for five years as pastor before he came to the United States. They had regular evangelistic series every month in their church; in most of those series, Maeda admitted, he was the evangelist. He now recognized that for five years he was preaching American sermons in Japan! He learned all his theology from Western textbooks—practical theology, systematic theology, as he went through seminary. Most all of his models were western models. Now when he looked back he felt embarrassed, but was grateful to God for what he had done in spite of him. Now he is a tremendously effective and successful preacher of the Gospel. That's what can happen to a national, to the respondent when he starts to become aware of his own culture.

Change in the sending church and its leadership. Finally, consider what can happen right here in our churches and in our educational institutions if we properly balance what is involved in level two and three of the Berger paradigm. Last week I was in Florida all week at a conference and someone came up to me and said, "You know, we've got a problem in our church. we can take an offering for displaced persons or people coming from other cultures and we get a tremendous response, but when we try to encourage our Christians who give liberally to invite these foreign people in for coffee, it doesn't happen. What's the problem?" Think of what can happen in our churches when we begin to understand that one of the ways to relate to those of other cultures is to become *learners* instead of insisting that we always be the *teachers.* Whole new vistas of communication will open up; psychological barriers will be broken down. And we become true emissaries of our Lord. In this context I would like to address myself especially to the evaluators at that third level, to the theologians in the large sense of that word, to the academicians, to our school people. I'm bothered. We have scores of young people at my seminary who have dedicated themselves to Christian mission, but most often I hear them come and say something like this, when I ask them what would you like to do, what would you like to be in the Third World or wherever it might be? "A teacher, a teacher," they say, and I know they're not ready. A better answer to that question is, a learner, a pupil, and then a teacher.

I wonder if we've listened to those Third World contextualization-conscious theologians who framed the Seoul Declaration when they said:

Western theology is by and large rationalistic, molded by Western philosophies, preoccupied with intellectual concerns, especially those having to do with faith and reason. All too often, it has reduced the Christian faith to abstract concepts which may have answered the questions of the past, but which fail to grapple with the issues of today. It has consciously been conformed to the secularistic world-view associated with the Enlightenment. . . . Furthermore, having been wrought in Christendom, it hardly addresses the questions of people living in situations characterized by religious pluralism, secularism, resurgent Islam, or Marxist totalitarianism. . . . Consequently, we insist on the need for critical reflection and theological renewal. We urgently need an Evangelical theology which is faithful to Scripture and relevant to the varied situations in the Third World.[16]

Consider the case of Morris Inch, formerly of Wheaton College Graduate School, who has taken the contextualization challenge seriously. Instead of going to Africa to teach only, he went to learn while teaching. Instead of delivering Wheaton lectures intact and unchanged, he kept asking questions of African students enmeshed in a world-view in which spirits abounded, in which the power encounter took precedence over the truth encounter. Inch has become a different kind of theologian. His recent books, *Doing Theology Across Cultures*[17] and *Making the Message Relevant*[18] introduce us to a systematic theologian who is attempting to aid believing communities in other cultures as well as his own. And growing and becoming a better instructor of budding Western theologues in the process!

As a missionary, a missiologist, I challenge you, wherever you sit and however you relate to these three levels that we have spoken of, to give new thought to the relationship between the Christian faith and culture. Theologians can now in a new way become our allies in the missionizing task, if only they will. It will mean a change in some of those time-honored notes from which they have discoursed for lo these many years in order to answer the questions of internationals who might be listening, who might be in the classroom and who have different sorts of questions and may not be overly-enthused about the difference between supralapsarianism and infralapsarianism and the distinction between three seeds in the Spirit and two seeds. It may mean taking the time at some juncture to actually go as a missionary-theologian and to learn and teach in another culture. It will mean helping us in this process of sorting out the cultural from the super-cultural and in responding to the excessive statements of those who become overly-converted to the social sciences.

Conclusion

I used to think of the New Jerusalem—the City of God—as being the antithesis of the Old Babylon, altogether in one place with one voice praising the Redeemer, but I now believe that such a view overlooks an important dimension. The cultural diversity that accrued to the dispersion from Babel is not forgotten in God's City, but will constitute an important aspect of the praise that will accrue to our Christ.

Thou was slain and didst purchase for God with Thy blood
men from every tribe and tongue and people and nation.
And Thou has made them to be a kingdom and priests to our
God; and they will reign upon the earth (Rev. 9b-10).

By the time we arrive in the New Jerusalem both the Cultural and the Gospel mandates will have been carried out. It is against the kaleidoscope of cultural, ethnic, and linguistic diversity that the unity of the heavenly community will be prized. It is the conjoining of that diversity and that unity that brings the ultimate praise to our God and Savior. And it is participation in cross-cultural ministry today that not only presages that multi-cultural community of praise in heaven, but that, under God, makes it possible. In a way now never achieved and seldom appreciated apart from Spirit-inspired bridging and celebrations, that building and those celebrations presage a time when the kaleidoscopic differences of earth conjoin to produce the magnitude and magnificence of doxological unity in heaven. Thank you.

1. I. Howard Marshall, "Culture and the New Testament" in John Stott and Robert T. Coote, eds., *Gospel and Culture* (Pasadena, Calif: William Carey Library, 1979), p. 27.
2. cf. David J. Hesselgrave, *Communicating Christ Cross-Culturally* (Grand Rapids: Zondervan Publishing House, 1978).
3. Donald J. Bloesch, *Crumbling Foundations: Death and Rebirth in an Age of Upheaval* (Grand Rapids: Zondervan Publishing House [Academic Books], 1984), pp. 122-124.
4. Paul J. Hiebert, "Critical Contextualization" *International Bulletin of Missionary Research, Vol. II, No. 3 (July, 1987), p. 104.*
5. *Quoted in Hiebert, ibid, p. 104.*
6. Peter Berger and Thomas Luckman, *The Social Construction of Reality* (Garden City, N.Y.: Doubleday, 1966), pp. 1-3.
7. Peter Beyerhaus, for example, is critical of the very idea of an "autonomous"

church in view of the fact that the Biblical teaching is that the church is "Christonomous"—everywhere and always under the rulership of Christ. See Peter Beyerhaus and Henry Lefever, *The Responsible Church and the Foreign Mission* (Grand Rapids: William B. Eerdmans, 1964), pp. 112 f.

8. Cf. James O. Buswell, III, "Contextualization: Theory, Tradition, and Method" in David J. Hesselgrave, ed. *Theology and Mission: Papers Given at Trinity Consultation No. 1* (Grand Rapids: Baker Book House, 1978), pp. 87-106; and Bruce C.E. Fleming, *Contextualization of Theology: An Evangelical Assessment* (Pasadena: William Carey Library, 1980).

9. Charles Kraft, *Christianity in Culture* (Maryknoll, N.Y.:Orbis Books, 1979), cf. especially pp. 130-142.

10. Harvie M. Conn, *Eternal Word and Changing Worlds: Theology, Anthropology and Mission in Trialogue* (Grand Rapids: Zondervan Publishing Col., [Academic Books], 1984), cf. especially pp. 315-338.

11. Donald A. McGavran, *The Bridges of God* (N.Y.: Friendship Press, 1955).

12. Quoted in James O. Buswell, III, "Contextualization: Is it only a new word for indigenization?", *Evangelical Missions Quarterly,* Vol. 14, No. 1 (January, 1978), p. 18.

13. H.R. Weber, *The Communication of the Gospel to Illiterates* (Madras: The Christian Literature Society, 1960).

14. Eizoh Maeda "A Study of the Evangelisitc Preaching of Selected American Evangelicals in an Attempt to Discover Evangelistic Preaching Principles which would be effective in Japanese Evangelism," (unpublished Master of Theology thesis, Trinity Evangelical Divinity School, 1971).

15. Maeda, ibid., p. 154.

16. "The Seoul Declaration: Toward an Evangelical Theology for the Third World" in Bong Rin Ro and Ruth Eshenauer, eds., *The Bible and Theology in Asian Contexts* (Taichung, Taiwan: Asian Theological Association, 1984), p. 23.

17. Morris Inch, *Doing Theology Across Cultures,* (Grand Rapids: Baker Book House, 1982).

18. Morris Inch, *Making the Good News Relevant: Keeping the Gospel Distinctive in Any Culture* (Nashville: Thomas Nelson, 1986).

EUGENE W. BUNKOWSKE, Ph. D.

Dr. Bunkowkse is chairman of the Pastoral Ministry Department at Concordia Theological Seminary and Director of Mission Education. Before coming to the Seminary as Professor of Missions in 1982, he served as a missionary in Africa for 22 years. He has also worked as translations coordinator for the United Bible Societies for the continent of Africa. During his years in Africa, he lived in Nigeria, and Kenya. He has translated or helped to translate the Scriptures into many African languages. He received an M. Div. from Concordia Seminary, St. Louis in 1960, the M.A., C. Phil., and Ph. D. degrees from U. C. L. A., the last in 1976, and in 1983 Concordia College, Winfield, Kansas awarded him a Doctor of Letters degree. He has lectured and conducted workshops and Seminars in over half of the countries of Africa and in many other parts of the world. His *Topics in Yala Grammar* is recognized as making an outstanding contribution in the field of linguistics with respect to the analysis of tone and eliding boundaries. He lives on campus at Ft. Wayne with his wife Bernice; they have four children.

COMMUNICATING CHRIST TO THE YALA PEOPLE

Eugene W. Bunkowske, Ph. D.

Introduction

The third annual Missions Congress is dedicated to communications from the point of view of those who do the communicating. We have considered God as the communicator both in terms of the Old Testament and the New Testament Model. We have considered what it means to communicate across linguistic and cultural space.

This evening gives us a chance to look into God's communicators from a case study point of view, that is, by actually tasting and feeling what it is like to communicate Christ to a people in another part of the world with a different way of viewing reality and a different way of talking about what is perceived to be real and true.

The Geographic Context

When you think of the Yala people you have necessarily to think of Africa because that is where the Yalas live. The land area of Africa is large enough to contain the U. S. A., India, Argentina, Europe, New Zealand, and China, with 38,000 square miles to spare. This land area is divided into 52 different nation states with between 1,500 and 2,000 different languages and approximately two and a half times (580,000,000) as many people as live in the United States of America.

Nigeria, with its artificial boundaries and sharp cultural differences, was a creation of the British Empire. It is the most populous nation of Africa, with approximately 100,000,000 inhabitants. In 1885, the Berlin Conference recognized Britain's claim to the Niger basin. Already in 1861 Britain had annexed the settlement of Lagos as a colony. Not until 1914 were Lagos, the northern protectorate and the southern protectorate amalgamated into the "Colony and Protectorate of Nigeria." The present boundaries of Nigeria were not fixed until 1960. It is estimated that in 1930 5% of the people in Nigeria were Christians. Today 46% of the Nigerian population is Christian.

In the midst of the 100 million Nigerians there are approximately 100,000 Yala people. The Yalas live in the eastern part of Nigeria, south of the Benue River in an area known as Ogoja. They enjoy their own special language, culture, and land area in the midst of 394 other Nigerian languages and some 500 to 700 distinct cultural groups.

Although the Yala nation in Ogoja was officially, at least from the point of view of the European powers, a part of Nigeria and under British rule since about 1900, there was little contact between the British and the Yalas until after the First World War (1914-1918). It was not until after World War II (1945) that the Ogoja area was really integrated into the rest of the country.

The Mission Background

Already in 1935 Dr. Nau, who was one of the first Synodical Conference Missionaries in Nigeria, suggested starting mission work in Ogoja. Finally in the late 1950's missionaries went north from the Efik-speaking area to Ogoja. Among the first to go were Ottermoeller, Winter, Lail, and Watkins. In 1961, my wife and I were asked to follow them for the specific purpose of opening work in western Yala by building a hospital at Yahe.

The Word Heard and Believed

One of the early remembrances that I have of Ogoja is going to Alebo and speaking the Word of God through an interpreter, having all the people run away, and finally having the chief come out. He seemed to want to find out what I was saying. With the help of an interpreter, I was able to share the Word of God with him and unbeknownst to me also with his people who were hiding behind the nearby trees and bushes. The chief was visibly shaking and anxious for me to leave. It was years later that I learned that our coming to Yala had been preceded by a rumor that the "white devil" was coming. What a way to start!

How then does a person communicate Christ to a people in a strange and uncertain situation like this?

Instead of sharing the story with you chronologically, I would like to move forward to some of the breakthroughs and then go back to fill in the false starts and stumblings along the way. Certainly what finally transpired was nothing but God's bountiful grace in action, as He used "common clay pots" to carry out His marvelous work.

We had tried many things. We had spoken to many people about God's love in Christ in English. Finally, after a number of difficult experiences and after the hospital was built, Bernice, our four children, and I found ourselves moving to Okpoma. Okpoma is in central Yala. It is the town where the clan chief, the tribal chief of all of the Yala people, lives. We found ourselves living in a rented house there, recognizing that we had to learn the language and above all reduce it to writing. We needed somehow to be able to communicate to people in a way that they could understand.

Now the chief had been very kind to us and given us a place to live, and so I felt that he should be one of the first people with whom I would talk and work. Chief Ogipwole had been chief for some 47 years.

Almost daily he would go to the court, which was approximately a mile from his palace. In order to reach the court, Chief Ogipwole would pass our house and we would share a friendly morning greeting with him. The people were always waiting for him as he approached the court. They knew that if they treated him right they would get the judgments that they wanted. This means that often before the court session started he would be well lubricated and easily prompted to make the desired judgments. After the court session was over, the chief would normally find his way home in a kind of erratic fashion. He normally stopped at our home. He would come in and say, "Nobe! (Greetings) Ada! (Respected one!)." Then he would promptly sit down and fall asleep. After an hour or two, he would wake up and go home.

My wife and I had a disagreement about this situation. I remember Bernice saying, "Gene, you know, how can this be a good witness? The chief comes every day; he is drunk every time. What kind of a witness is that anyway?" So we had a little difference of opinion over him. I insisted that we should be hospitable to the chief and Bernice yielded.

Time passed and one day the chief came to me and said, "I was known as a very wise chief when I was young. Now it is different. I know the people are laughing at me behind my back. What should I do?" I thought for a moment and then said to him almost immediately, without really considering it, "Chief, you and I need to make a covenant with each other, a bargain that we will no longer drink any kaikai." Kaikai is the most alcoholic drink in Yala. You could use it for lighting a fire. Then I repeated, "I think we should make a bargain not to touch kaikai at all." The chief agreed and said, "I will try." This single action changed things for Chief Ogipwole in a tremendous way. Now when he went to the court he was clear-minded. He had 40-plus years of experience behind him, and once again he gave correct and just judgments.

He continued to stop by each day. One time instead of sitting down where I was working with Ferdinand Oji on Bible translation, he went around and sat in our living room. My wife Bernice went in to talk to the chief. All at once, she burst into my study. She took the little brass cross off of my desk and the next thing Mr. Oji and I knew she was speaking to Chief Ogipwole and she was saying, "You know there is a God that made all the world and He took His own son and He put him on the cross-stick (that's the word we use for the cross of Christ in Yala) and He sacrificed Him there so that we never, ever will have to sacrifice again."

About that time, Ferdinand and I realize what Bernice was doing. As she concluded her brief witness by saying, "The Son of God was put in the ground and after three days came out again," Ferdinand and I joined them in the sitting room. I read from the Scripture that Ferdinand and I had just been translating and we spoke more about the meaning of the Gospel. When we finished, the chief said not a word. He just got up and went home. As far as I knew, nothing at all had changed, and nothing had happened. In the days to come, I often spoke to Chief Ogipwole of God's love and forgiveness. It just seemed as though it never got through at all.

About a month later, things turned in another direction. This is how it always seemed to be. At least this is how it was for us in our mission work. I would make plans about what I thought should be done, and in most cases God would take us off in quite a different direction.

It all started when a group of men were going with me to a funeral ceremony. They were all men of my age group. In Yala you, by definition, have your closest friendship and fellowship with the people who are approximately your same age. In fact, the age companies are formally grouped and organized. Since burial is the most important thing in an African's life and since African life is communal, you cannot go to a funeral alone. You must go with your friends and age-mates.

Now back to the chief. Just as we were about to leave for the burial, my friends and I, here came Chief Ogipwole. He said, "I'm going with you." Well, we knew very well that a paramount chief normally does not go to funerals. Particularly if the corpse is there, he must certainly not be present. Fortunately, in this case, the corpse had already been buried.

In any case, the chief went along. As we got there, no sooner did we get out from my VW van than the sub-chief and the local elders came up to us in amazement and rage. They said, "Ogipwole, what are you doing here? You should not be here." My age-mates tried to explain. One said, "The chief is old. He can forget. Please forgive him." Others tried other excuses. No excuse was accepted. There would be no forgiveness. Finally, each one had exhausted all of his ideas for appeasing the wrath of the sub-chief and the local elders.

Then the chief himself stood up to speak. Now I was really wondering what would happen. He started to berate the people of Itega Ukpudu in a loud and angry voice. "Aren't you my people? Are you people totally stupid? Don't you understand anything?"

By this time I thought, "Boy, are we ever in trouble." I still did not fully comprehend what the basic problem was. Now as the chief spoke, it became clear. They were accusing him of coming without one of his official counselors. The point was that a paramount chief has up to three formally appointed counselors. He may leave his palace and go out of town, but he must, by law, take at least one of the formally appointed counselors with him so that he won't sell the land or in some way make an unwise decision for the entire tribe. And so here the chief was five miles from his palace without a counselor. They had him dead to rights as far as all of us could see. Finally, after about twenty minutes of berating them, Chief Ogipwole looked straight at his accusing sub-chief and said, "Here is my counselor." At the same time, he pointed at me. At that moment it was as if a thunder-bolt had hit the place. Everyone seemed to simultaneously realize that a paramount Yala chief has the right to have three formal counselors and that he also has the right to appoint them. Since, in fact, there was a vacancy because of the death of one of the official counselors a year before, there was a natural vacancy to be filled.

As you can imagine, the news went up and down the Yala countryside like wild fire. No one even thought to say, "It's funny that this counselor has a different kind of face and background than the other two." Rather, everyone marvelled at the wisdom of the chief and spoke highly of his choice and of the fact that the cocky elders and the sub-chief from Itega Ukpudu had been bested in the contest of wits. Now things really started to move. About three weeks later, Chief Ogipwole came to me and said, "You are my counselor, aren't you?" I said, "Yes!" He said, "I am going out to install a new sub-chief in eastern Yala. Will you come with me?" I agreed and we went.

There we were sitting under the trees. Around us were about 5,000 people, including the district officer, government officials, and many visitors from the neighboring tribes. There were many speakers, the last of which was Chief Ogipwole. He spoke last because he was the oldest and the most respected of all the chiefs in that area. He got up and said, "You all know that I am going to give the genealogy of this young man whom we want to make chief today. You heard about that earlier today, how very, very important it is that this man comes from the right family. But contrary to your expectations, I am not going to go through the genealogy again today. The elders have carefully checked his family tree and we all know that we would not be here today if the man we are about to crown as a sub-chief were not from the right family. I am not going to repeat the genealogy because I have something that is even more important to say."

This then is the chief's speech: "This new sub-chief will not build all of the big shrines in front of his palace that I did when I became a chief. He must know, as I now do know, that there is only one God that made all of the world. That God is the creator of all the nations. Not only of the Yalas, but also of the Kukeles, the Bokis, and even of the people of the United States where this my counselor comes from. This new sub-chief and all of you people must realize that this God loves us and that He has sent His own Son into this world. You must also realize that this great God sacrificed his only Son on the cross-stick so that we would never have to sacrifice again. After God's Son died, He was put in the ground."

What joy it was for me to hear these words. You can be sure that I was listening and that I had tears in my eyes.

Then the chief went on. He said, "This Son of God was put in the ground and after seven days (I was about ready to say, "Chief, three days," but I guess the Lord put a cork in my mouth.) he then came out of the ground and came back to life." The chief then said, "When I go hunting, I'm going to go and be with the Son of God who died for me and rose again. No shrines or sacrifices are needed now because God has done it all for us in His Son."

The reason the chief spoke about going hunting is that it is believed that a Yala chief never dies but that he goes hunting and just never returns.

And there it was. There was the explosion for the opening up of the Gospel among the Yala people. That was in 1972. We had been among the Yala people for eleven years by that time. The point that I want to make here is that it comes in God's time and not according to our timetable. We may expect results in six months or in six days, but it may rather be eleven or twenty years. The point is that it took a long time. The hospital had been built by that time. We were tempted at times to leave, but God still had work for us to do, so we learned the language, translated the Scriptures, and witnessed through Word and deed.

The Word Misheard

To work with people of different languages and cultures means learning. It means learning how people with other ways of life look at the same world with a different focus. For them, different things are important and of primary concern. In fact, some of our most basic concepts may not be shared or perceived in the same way. We learned that very early on in Nigeria. We started in

Nigeria in the Efik-speaking area. My first assignment in 1960 was to be responsible for a district of 25 churches and 20 parochial schools. Each Sunday it was a different church with a full service including preaching, Lord's Supper, Baptism, confirmation, and often weddings and burials. Imagine doing that after you have been in a country for four weeks and you do not speak the language and you have to do everything through an interpreter.

I, for one, like to be able to understand what people are saying. Maybe I have always been a bit of a communicator and that was one of the most frustrating things I have known—to work through the interpreter. Imagine what it meant for me on a day down in Ekeya when a man came to me and he spoke English. What a joy to speak the Gospel directly to that man in English. I asked him, "Can you read English?" He said, "Yes!" I knew that I had a New Testament in my car. I got it. I gave him the New Testament and said, "This is the power of God unto salvation! Use it!" The man took the New Testament and we left. It had been a long day already with six hours of service.

It was 25 Sundays later that I got back to Ekeya. The first thing I could think of was, "I wonder about that man with the New Testament." And as I went through the service, I saw him sitting out there and I was so happy. When the service was over, I could not wait for him to shake my hand at the back of the church. I wanted to talk to him about the New Testament. As he approached me, I saw that he had the New Testament with him, and I said to him, "I see you have the New Testament; was it helpful to you?" "Oh," he said, "it was very, very helpful. You told me it was the power of God unto salvation." Then I took the New Testament from him and I looked at it. Immediately I saw that the cover was gone, Matthew was gone, and even part of Mark was gone. I said, "You really have used your New Testament, haven't you?" He said, "Yes, just like you told me." He said, "I'm a trader, I move around, buying and selling, and as I get into the vehicles of transport, I tear out one page and put it right down on the seat, and sit on it. Truly, just as you said, I was perfectly protected at all times."

What a shock to me! That is not what I had said. My eyes filled with tears because I realized that he heard with different ears. I had said that it is the power of God unto salvation, and he believed me. He took it literally in terms of an animistic understanding that there is always a physical representation of spiritual power. That the power is in the physical object itself.

This experience taught me about other world-views than my own. It helped me realize that people did not always perceive or understand what I intended for them to understand when I spoke or acted. They gave different meaning to my words and actions than the meaning which I had so carefully hoped to associate with those words and actions.

Then as we were asked to go to Ogoja, I remember thinking, "Now I'll do better." As we built the hospital at Yahe, I planned for an hour of Bible study with all of the workers each day. We did it first thing in the morning. We could do it in English because all of the workers could speak some pidgeon English, and so we were able to understand each other. By that time I also had learned to speak pidgeon English. And so we faithfully did the Bible study every day and within about four months every single one of the workers had received Christ Jesus as his Savior. Bernice and I rejoiced in seeing them "saved".

After about a year, the first buildings at the hospital had been completed. By that time, we had run out of money, and so we had to close down the building operation. This meant that the men had to go home. As I thought about it, I felt sorry for the men, but at the same time I saw it as a tremendous opportunity for them to witness to their families. In order to prepare for this, we spent the last several months before we closed down the building operation working through the Book of Acts to teach them about reaching out to others and witnessing.

After the workmen went home, I went down to Obot Idim, our mission headquarters, for some time to attend meetings. About two weeks later I returned and immediately went to visit the men to see what God had done through their witness. In my typical American style I was expecting "instant mashed potatoes." The first man that I visited was Odo. He was still unmarried and so he lived in his father's compound together with the rest of his extended family. The first thing I looked for was the family shrine. It was my hope that it would have been dismantled and destroyed. To my chagrin, it was still there. I was disappointed. I wondered what Odo had said and done. Maybe he had neglected to witness. Instead of asking a lot of questions I recognized that it had been a short time and that being dependent on his father he might not have been in a very good position to make his points of witness stick. I enjoyed foods and fellowship with Odo and his father and family. Odo and his people were very cordial.

As I went home, I decided to visit Odama next, since I knew that he was a more respected and somewhat older man who was intending to get married in the not too distant future. When I got to Odama's compound, Odama had, in fact, married. He had saved the money which he had earned at the medical center, and added it to the money which his father had saved for the wedding of his son, and had used this money to pay the dowry of his bride. As a married man, he had set up his own separate little compound, but near to the compound where his father lived. I immediately surmised that here would be the ideal situation since Odama could now set up his own separate life and obviously he and his new bride would be model Christians. With this in mind, we walked out of his father's compound and what should I see in front of Odama's newly-built home but a huge pagan shrine. I thought, "How can this be?" I said, "Odama, what have you done? What do you have that shrine in front of your house?" Odama said, "Christianity is all right over there at the Medical Center on the land that the chief and elders gave to you for your god. Jesus Christ is all right there, but out here among the Yala people, in Yala land, there are different spiritual powers. If I don't put up a shrine, my wife will be barren and my yams will not grow."

Again, I was brought up short. I stopped and thought. Again, I realized that the Yala people hear with different ears and see with different eyes. All at once I understood the point. I knew the words. I could give the right definitions in the seminary, but here things were different. It hit me when Odama said, "We gave the land to you, that's where your god is. This is the land of our gods." All at once I understood polytheism. Many gods, each connected with a certain land area, each controlling his own space. How different it is here in the U. S. A. with monotheism in place. This is true even of the atheist and the agnostic. Although the atheist or the agnostic would reject the idea of a personal God or gods yet, if for the sake of discussion, you postulate the idea of God and ask, "How many gods are there?" The answer from the atheist would almost certainly be, one. His underlying basis for understanding is monotheistic. For the traditional African, it is just the opposite. He has a polytheistic world view from very early in life. How then do we break through with clear communication when the basic presuppositions and assumptions are so different?

These insights led me to realize that we had to move closer to the people in order to really understand their culture and the associated Yala language. When the hospital building was finished we moved out to Okpoma. There we really got to know the people and the chief. As the communication barriers were cleared away, Chief Ogipwole and many others really heard the Word of God in such a way that the Holy Spirit worked saving faith in their mind, hearts, and lives. As they received Jesus as their personal Savior, the work of witness broke out among the people and the Holy Spirit brought more and more to faith in Jesus.

The Word of God Moves out through Bible Translation

When it came to language analysis and Bible translation, I worked with Mr. Ferdinand Ogi in the same way that I had worked with others. We began with no less than an hour and in most cases two hours of Bible study every day and then we turned to the work of the analysis of the language, setting up of a writing system, and working toward Bible translation. After about four years there came a time when we were ready to start with the actual Bible translation. At that point, I wondered, "Where shall we start?"

One day I sort of spontaneously asked Ferdinand, "Where shall we start our translation, with which book of the Bible? Should it be Genesis, Matthew, or where?" I put it this way, "What if we should live just long enough to do one book of the Bible, then which book of the Bible should it be?" In our study we had touched on every book of the Bible and so I knew Ferdinand would be thinking about the whole corpus of Scripture before he answered my question. I did not expect an immediate answer, because Ferdinand often would take several days to answer a question like this. To my surprise, Ferdinand answered immediately. He looked at me and said, "The book that we will have to translate first has got to be Jonah!" I was shocked and automatically responded, "Ferdinand, why Jonah?" Back in those days as you well remember the book of Jonah was very much questioned by critical scholarship and certainly would not have been most people's first choice. So I guess it is no wonder that I so quickly asked, "Why Jonah?"

Ferdinand's answer was most enlightening. He said, "Well, you know that we Yala people believe that there is one kind of spiritual power in Yala, another kind of spiritual power in Kukele, and yet another in Boki. Every tribe has its own gods and a separate source of spiritual power. The book of Jonah teaches us that even when Jonah wanted to run away from God outside of his own land area and go over the Mediterranean Sea to Spain God was there. God was everywhere." He was seeing Jonah wherever he went. The book of Jonah tells us that when the big storm came, the sailors said, "Jonah, is it your God that is angry at you?" Jonah said, "Yes, it is!" They threw Jonah overboard and immediately the storm stopped. Then we read an interesting thing about these pagan sailors. The sailors themselves worshipped Yahweh. Ferdinand said, "The second point that we learn from the book of Jonah is that all people can worship that God, not only the Jews, but people all over the world can worship that God. We, too, the Yala people can worship that God." Then Ferdinand went on to his third reason for choosing Jonah by pointing out that when Jonah got put inside of the whale and then was thrown out on to the beach, we see that God has a purpose for every person in the world. We're not here for nothing. And finally, Ferdinand's fourth point for choosing Jonah was that God is a God of grace and when people repent like the people of Nineveh repented, then God is ready to forgive.

The fact that Ferdinand Oji gave me that immediate response without going home to ponder over it told me that God had already moved him to do a lot of thinking about what message the Yala people needed to hear and which part of Scripture put it in a way that they could easily understand.

The clarity of Ferdinand's first response led me to ask again. I suppose in all honesty that although Ferdinand's logic for the choice of Jonah was very clear I had hoped for a New Testament book, preferably a Gospel. So I said, "Ferdinand, what if we live long enough to do two books, which one should be second?" It wasn't long before he said, "There's no choice. The second one has got to be Hebrews! You know how much we spend on sacrifices. The Yala people spend 25 per cent to 50 per cent of their money on sacrifices. That is why the book of Hebrews will be such good news indeed." Ferdinand then turned to Hebrews 10:10 and read, "Because Jesus Christ did what God wanted him to do, we are all purified from sin by the offering that he made of his own body once and for all." Then without any further questions from me, Ferdinand continued, "After that, the Yala people are going to be asking us, 'Who is Jesus Christ?' and after that we can translate the Gospel of Luke and the Book of Acts. Luke will tell the Yala people who Jesus is and Acts will show the Yala people how the early church took the message of repentance and forgiveness in Jesus Christ to all the world. If we get that much done, then it won't matter too much if we die."

The Lord is very good. The Yala New Testament is now complete. It has been printed and is in use. At this point certain other portions of the Old Testament are being worked on. Some are already in print and being utilized. And so the Word of God moves out through Bible translation.

The Word Moves Out through Indigenous Music

As Ferdinand and I worked on Bible translation, I suppose he was much like Martin Luther. He just felt compelled to find a way for the message to move out. So almost immediately from the beginning Ferdinand took selected Scripture portions and put them to Yala music. Soon the children were singing that music in the playgrounds in the evening. Soon it moved out from Okpoma to other towns. From town to town as the Word of the Lord grew.

I knew very little about musicology. I was a bit worried when the people began to sing these songs all over Yala and so I said to Ferdinand one day, "How do you choose the music for these hymns?" By that time I understood the language well enough to know that there were songs about head-hunting and all kinds of songs, both bad and good. So I asked Ferdinand, "How do you choose the tunes?" Ferdinand said to me, "Well, there are some tunes that I do not use. When you hear that tune, then there are certain thoughts and ideas that are automatically connected with that musical tune. If those thoughts are non-Scriptural or against the

Word of God, I do not use that music. If the thought-connotations in the music is positive or neutral, I use that tune."

And there it was. The Word of God moved out through music. In every culture that I know, music is a powerful message-projector. If the proper indigenous music is chosen the capacity for the message to move out is much enhanced. If non-indigenous music is chosen, the natural movement of the Gospel is often repressed.

The Word Moves Out through Pastoral Training

One of the young Yala men took a great interest in God's Word right from the beginning. He had some initial training at the Bible school even before we moved to Okpoma. Today Matthias Odey is a national pastor in the Lutheran Church of Nigeria working among his own people. Some of the boys that were very close friends of our sons, Walter and Joel, while we lived at Okpoma are now lay preachers and evangelists. These lay preachers and evangelists work under the leadership of Reverend Odey. They have become very instrumental in carrying the Word of God to other parts of Yala land, where preaching stations and full congregations are now being formed.

Conclusion

And so the Church expands, and one station grows upon another. For our family, and particularly for Bernice and myself, it was something like being on the 50-yard line with the unique privilege of watching what God was doing. Truly God was doing it because so often our attempts led to nothing and something peripheral that wasn't part of my human plan or approach is what God used to break down the communications barriers so that the Word would be heard. Once the Word was heard then the Spirit of God was free to work and work he certainly did.

I would like to close by sharing Isaiah 55:8-11:

"My thoughts," says the Lord, "are not like yours, and my ways are different from yours. As high as the heavens are above the earth, so high are my ways and thoughts above yours. My word is like the snow and the rain that comes down from the sky to water the earth. It makes the crops grow and provides seed for sowing and food for eating. So also will be the Word that I speak—it will not fail to do what I plan for it; it will do everything I send it to do."

REV. WALLACE SCHULZ

Rev. Schulz has served as Associate Lutheran Hour speaker since April, 1977, during which time he has shared preaching duties with Dr. Oswald Hoffman on the weekly radio broadcast. Rev. Schulz was born and raised in Parkston, South Dakota. He received a B. S. from Concordia Teachers College, Seward, Nebraska and an M. Div. from Concordia Theological Seminary, Springfield, Illinois. He served on the faculty of Concordia College in Ann Arbor, Michigan from 1967-1969 and was an assistant pastor at St. Paul Lutheran Church in Sioux City, Iowa in 1973-4. He served on the staff of Concordia College, River Forest, Illinois from 1975 through 1977. He has participated in several world congresses on evangelism and in 1986 received the Ellis Island Medal of Honor. He and his wife Kathy life in a suburb of St. Louis.

Listeners to the Lutheran Hour will recognize Rev. Schulz's pungent style and forthright manner of speaking in the following paper, which is an expanded version of the one he delivered in Ft. Wayne on October 2, 1987.

THE ELECTRONIC MEDIA
"Can It Be Used Effectively For Evangelism-Missions?"

Rev. Wallace Schulz

"It is extremely difficult, if not impossible, to proclaim the Gospel through the use of television."[1] Does this sound like a statement by some disgruntled media critic? Hardly! This sincere and astounding evaluation was expressed by the famous British journalist Malcolm Muggeridge, after a half-century career of broadcast and print journalism.[2]

The majority of people today would most likely sneer, saying, "Aw c'mon, Muggeridge, where have you been for the last fifteen years? After all, anyone who watches even a little bit of television knows that there are 'some mighty powerful preachers' on television every week, and they have larger audiences than all the churches put together."[3]

Convincing? Perhaps. But let's take another look. Today, in the United States, we have 221 full-time television stations broadcasting religion. Now, please note carefully: these are not secular stations with an occasional half-hour religious program sandwiched into their Sunday format. These 221 television stations are devoted exclusively to religious broadcasting, often 24 hours a day. And, scattered over the United States are an additional 1,370 full-time religious radio stations; many of these broadcast religion day and night.[4]

However, we have a most unexpected dilemma. In a 1985 Gallup poll it was revealed that, in spite of the numerous American churches preaching religion each week plus the proliferation of religious radio and TV broadcasting, when people were asked what comes to mind when Jesus Christ is discussed, only 13 percent of all people surveyed replied that they associated the idea of forgiveness with the man called Jesus.[5] The majority of people considered Jesus primarily a great teacher, a great religious leader, or a spiritual guru: one to emulate if you desire to "do good" and to get to heaven. From this it would seem the American population is quite "religious" but not necessarily Christian; and that possibly media-religion is making very little impact!

Thus, before we automatically and enthusiastically jump on the bandwagon of using media as one of the best ways of proclaiming the Good News of forgiveness in Jesus Christ, perhaps we should take a closer look.

When it All Began

On January 2, 1921, the switch was thrown, and KDKA, Pittsburgh, carried a remote broadcast from Calvary Episcopal Church. Now, what most critics don't realize (especially those who currently cry that in recent years media-evangelists have been taking over the air waves) is that the first religious program was broadcast only two months after the first licensed commercial station went on the air.[6]

Equally interesting is the fact that, just as quickly as religion attached itself to secular broadcasting, so rapidly did controversy piggy-back both of them.[7] Honesty demands that some of the criticism has been a result of misunderstandings.

To understand the concept of the "Electronic Church," it is absolutely crucial to comprehend how evangelical and fundamentalist preachers perceive the use of media for evangelism.

Thus, as we examine the use of media as a tool for promoting the true Christian faith, we will benefit much from hearing briefly from several leading apologists of today's "electronic church;" and in order to provide windows of illumination on the subject, we shall listen carefully (but not always sympathetically) to respected critics. We shall raise several additional concerns unique to this group; we shall briefly examine the approach of the Roman Catholic church; and finally, we shall set forth the potential that God has given us for using the media in proclaiming Jesus Christ crucified, the only Hope of the world.

The majority of us gathered here today would probably be quite uncomfortable with the expression, "the radio church,"[8] or "the radio congregation,"[9] or the "radio pulpit."[10] As servants of the Word and loyal sons and daughters of the Reformation, we would understand the church or the congregation in a New Testament frame of reference: a public assembly of believers in Jesus Christ where the Word is proclaimed and the Sacraments are administered.[11] However, this thoroughly Scriptural concept of the church is shared neither by much of Protestantism nor by most of today's radio and television evangelists.[12]

Even though, for purposes of this discussion, setting forth the doctrine of the church would seem absolutely crucial to most of us, the vast majority of the leaders of the electric church would deem it as quite irrelevant. One who has, however, is Dr. Ben Armstrong in his widely read 1979 publication, *The Electric Church.*[13] Dr. Armstrong certainly does not speak for every 'media preacher;' yet, he has served for many years on the governing board of National Religious Broadcasters and has served also as its chairman. In his book Dr. Armstrong has assembled material solicited from major media-evangelistic organizations, both independent and those denominationally affiliated. Thus, his book serves as the most comprehensive source available in defense of the popular "electronic church" especially regarding its "philosophy," or "theology".

In his book, *The Electric Church,* Dr. Armstrong includes a chapter entitled, "Straight From the New Testament—A Revolutionary Idea." If one is to understand the popular phenomena of the electric church, this chapter is absolutely crucial. "The idea of the electric church," Dr. Armstrong explains, "came to me a few years ago on an airplane trip to Chicago. Weather conditions were very poor, the airplane was in a holding pattern, [and we circled] above Chicago for what seemed to be hours in total blackness. When the pilot finally received permission to land and the aircraft broke through the dense cloud cover, the lights of the city suddenly appeared below . . . thousands of sparkling pinpoints piercing the expansive blackness! . . . for the first time I saw the lights below, not as broadcasting towers, but as millions of broadcasting listeners and viewers; and I recognized them as members of **a great and new manifestation of the church created by God for this age—the electric church.**"[14]

Dr. Armstrong continues: "In the New Testament times, the members of the church gathered in homes. . . .[15] And in this . . . I saw the electric church as a revolutionary new form of worshiping, [like] the church that existed 20 centuries ago." In his opinion this is also a step toward the restoration of New Testament Christianity. "Radio and television," he states, "have broken through the walls of tradition we have built up over the church and have restored conditions remarkably similar to the early church."[16]

Armstrong then confesses: "At the time of my discovery of the electric church concept . . . only then did I grasp the authentic meaning of what God is doing with the electronic media."[17] Of course, this opens a real "Pandora's box" regarding where the real "church" exists, especially when Armstrong goes on to explain that a "study suggests there may be as many as 15 million Americans who do not belong to a church but are believers with an active faith, including prayer and Bible reading. Since these people are not attending church," Dr. Armstrong concludes, "some of them must be drawing spiritual support from the ministry of religious radio and television."

While for some this type of "alibi" for the "unchurched" may seem an adequate explanation, giving any type of approval to this view seems highly questionable at best. An even more dubious attitude is now widely held by many and was also reflected in an article which appeared in the August 30, 1987, issue of the *Minneapolis Star and Tribune*. In its lead, front page article, this paper noted that "Minnesotans have a far deeper religious faith than such common measures as church membership and attendance might indicate. They overwhelmingly believe there is a God who watches over humankind and responds to prayer. But those beliefs don't always result in going to church, praying, or reading the Bible." Indeed, Dr. Armstrong would certainly not totally support the Minnesota newspaper article; but isn't it safe to say that condoning worship at home in front of the television is only a small step from finally concluding that no special worship whatsoever is needed: everything one does (or doesn't do) is worship?

Thus, some of this may sound a bit disturbing to us. Nevertheless, honesty demands that we recognize that Dr. Armstrong does include statements such as: "The electric church is not a replacement for the local assembly . . . the electric church and the local church are different manifestations of the one church of Jesus Christ."[18]

While these expressions may seem "correct" theologically, most people would probably concur that after reading Armstrong's entire book, the overwhelming impression is that the author has sort of "tacked on" the idea of keeping the connection between religious media and the local church in order to try to minimize criticism.

If all this sounds a bit different from what you expected regarding the thinking of evangelical and fundamentalist media preachers, then you might be interested to know that this concept of the radio and television congregations was set forth, and was well received, at an annual gathering of the Religious Broadcasters in Washington D.C. After his presentation Armstrong wrote that he felt the reception to his idea "seemed good."[19]

In addition to this new understanding of the church, one may be further intrigued by the way some of the "electric church" view modern technology as a fulfillment of prophecy. This is interestingly depicted by a story involving the President of Evangelical Broadcasting in Holland, Dr. Glashower. Dr. Glashower said that when the famous Pentecostal apologist, Dr. David Du Plessis, met Karl Barth, Barth observed, "If you're so sure that the Bible predicts the future, why aren't radio and television there?" Du Plessis is said to have answered, "They are. Look at Revelation 14:6-7.[20] Revelation 14:6 reads: "And I saw another angel flying in midheaven, having an eternal Gospel to preach to those who live on the earth, and to every nation and tribe and tongue and people."

Dr. Armstrong seems to share somewhat the same idea regarding prophecy, and he certainly echoes the feelings of other evangelists[21] of the electronic church as he poses the question: "Is it possible that the angel specified in Revelation 14:6 is a heavenly body weighing 4,700 pounds, measuring 15 feet in length and 8 feet in width, and flying in geosynchronous orbit 22,000 miles above the earth?"[22]

Finally, Dr. Armstrong observes: "Only in recent years has it become possible technologically for a heavenly body to 'fly in the midst of heaven' with a message for those who dwell on the earth. With several communication satellites in operation today, it does not seem altogether unreasonable to assume that the communication satellite **may become the fulfillment of the prophesy of John who saw the vision of the author of the 'other angel' almost 2,000 years ago.**"[23]

To some of us, this kind of thinking may seem a bit unusual. These are ideas not likely taught at Concordia Theological Seminary in its classes on Revelation, communication, or preaching. However, for purposes of this presentation, the point is this: **Having this information helps us understand the zeal behind the current evangelical media missionary force**[24] which has caused the fundamentalist/evangelical movement to concentrate so heavily on media-evangelism that the *Washington Journalism Review* reported: "A new Christian-owned radio station is established every 7 days, and every 30 days a new Christian-owned religious television station appears."[25]

Lutheran Understanding of the Church and the role of Media

While a significant number of "Lutherans" embrace evangelical and fundamentalist theology and its view of the media,[26] we in the Confessional Lutheran Church have traditionally viewed the use of the media in religion from a different perspective. The primary purpose is to bring the gospel of Jesus Christ to anyone who cares to listen. In this context, we say that instead of using technology to promote home worship or home churches, we have attempted to make use of the media's potential for vast coverage and also of its ability to enter places normally inaccessible by the local congregation as a tool to locate evangelism prospects.

After hearing "The Lutheran Hour" or "This is The Life" people often respond by writing to one of our 21 offices around the world.[27] When these inquiries arrive in our Counseling Department, they immediately receive a letter of encouragement. And for all inquirers who appear to be an evangelism prospect, their names are sent to local pastors for follow-up; this procedure is used for this reason: **the local congregations (and not the television or radio congregation) are the institutions ordained by God** where He gathers people for Himself and nurtures them through the spoken and visible Word, for the strengthening of their faith and salvation of their souls.

Criticism of the Electric Church

Sporadic criticism of the electronic church has appeared in publications of most denominations;[28] and spokesmen of some of the more liberal churches appear to be the most scathing.[29] It is interesting to note that several of the largest Protestant bodies openly acknowledge that the reason they are not finally entering the media-evangelism arena is not so much to evangelize, (or to carry out the Great Commission) as much as it is to counteract[30] the overall influence of the evangelical/fundamentalist use of media[31] which they consider irritating and even dangerous.[32] One mainline Protestant church, the Episcopal Church, in its attempt to curb the evangelical/fundamentalist media influence, has even tried clever ads such as: "In a church started by a man who had six wives, forgiveness goes without saying."[33]

As criticism of the electric church gained momentum, there appeared in 1984 a book by Peter G. Horsfield entitled *Religious Television—The American Experience.* Many consider this book a benchmark work of liberal criticism of media-evangelism.[34] And while we may not agree with the theological stance of liberal churchmen such as Horsfield, we can frequently learn from them as we carefully examine their criticism.

For six years, Horsfield, while on leave from a Massachusetts Methodist pastorate and studying for a doctor's degree at Boston University Graduate School, gathered information for his book. He was assisted by members of the prestigious Annenberg School of Communications of the University of Pennsylvania; William Fore, a member of the National Council of Churches Communication Commission also assisted him;[35] and Mr. Robert White of the Center for the Study of Communication and Culture in London served as chief editor of the book. Horsfield's book is a well-documented work and would certainly be recommended to any student interested in a critical evaluation of media-evangelism.

Horsfield raises a number of issues which no responsible implementors of media-evangelism can avoid. His first criticism is one which media-evangelists and broadcasters have shouldered from the beginning and have never been able to effectively shake. "Broadcasters," he says, "try to give the impression that they are working diligently to assist the local church, even to the point of getting their viewers to start worshiping locally, and to discontinue their 'religious television' habit. However, research indicates otherwise." Horsfield notes: ". . . broadcasters make little effort to establish personal contact between respondents to their programs and a local church, though they frequently claim to be supportive of the idea."

Horsfield then further explains, ". . . following an inquiry about conversion to five paid-time religious broadcasters, a total of 54 mailings were received; [then] in the following nine month period only six of the return mailings were directed to answering the original inquiry; the remainder were directed primarily to fund solicitation by the broadcasters." Thus he concludes, "Suggestions that the inquirers become involved in the life of the local church were minimal and none of the broadcasters referred the inquirer's name to a local church for subsequent follow-up."[36]

Another legitimate concern expressed is: "Counseling materials sent [out] . . . place little or no stress on the need to become involved in a local church, and few referrals of inquirers are made. A content study of 15 paid-time religious programs by Hilton in 1980 found that in none of them was the local church ever mentioned! This was also true even for Robert Schuller, even though it is claimed of Schuller that he frequently encourages his television audience to attend a local church."[37]

So Horsfield observes: "While Schuller may incorporate other opportunities to delve more deeply into the content and implications of the Christian faith through his local church program at Garden Grove, television viewers receive none of this information, either through the television program or the direct mail follow-up. What remains unspoken in all of this is that the 'real caring' of which Schuller speaks is actually a staged, edited program which the preacher developed according to the demands of good television."[38]

A third criticism raised is that "few [new] members are brought into the church by religious programs on television,[39] and that increases in membership in the particular churches are due primarily either to the establishment of personal contact by another member of that congregation or by movement from other churches.[40] This is called "rechanneling" or, simply, changing churches.

In addition, it is also fascinating to see that, "When persons watching television are motivated to change their attitude toward religious faith, even to make a religious commitment of some sort, most frequently they integrate that decision into their existing environment rather than changing their environment.[41] (This means that, in a situation where a Roman Catholic would watch a Lutheran program in which "grace" is emphasized, this Roman Catholic viewer is merely stimulated to a greater commitment to the Roman Catholic church and its understanding of grace. Thus actually changing a fundamental religious concept in the mind of a listener is a rare accomplishment for most media programs.)[42] Furthermore, "A religious program on television may be effective in awakening within viewers dissatisfaction[43] with their present situation, prompting them to begin seeking a satisfying answer to newly aroused questions and needs."[44] While media-apologists like Armstrong admit this, they counter by pointing out that people change churches because the original one was not preaching the Word of God.[45] (While this may be true in some situations, in the vast majority of cases it would probably not be the case.)

Dr. Carl F.Henry, in the January 1980 issue of *Christianity Today,* raised probably the most serious issue regarding the electric church when he stated that the religious use of the mass media is often a "destructive trend which neglects a systematic teaching of Christian truth."[44] In April, 1984, *U.S. News & World Report* also noted: "Political issues are discussed in more than half the programs, while complicated theological issues are rarely debated." [47] The reason, of course, is born out by the fact that religious television programmers have tried to accommodate themselves to the Comstock finding that "Television within American society principally serves two social functions: that of entertainment[48] and killing time."[49]

Knowing this, one can also further understand why critics have astutely observed that religious programs must be constantly changing or looking for something novel in order to attract and maintain the viewer's attention.[50] As a consequence of this increased pressure, there has developed a regular cadre of religious program guests who move in a circuit from one program to another—Pat Boone, Dale Evans and Roy Rogers, Chuck

Colson, Ephram Zimbalist, Jr. All of them fulfill admirably the desired qualities of being well-known celebrities who also have the experience of something sensational that can be shared. With this in mind one is not surprised that "Christian theologians have begun to develop an interest in the content of the Christian television programs for reasons of evaluations. The concern expressed is that the current religious programs, in accommodating themselves to the demands of commercial television have lost the essence of the Christian message and have simply become indistinguishable facsimiles of other commercial television programs."[51]

Most media-evangelists are under considerable pressure to tailor their message so as not to offend viewers; consequently, most programs spend most of their time either in light entertainment or rehearsing the great sins of society; then, at the very end, they sort of "tack on" a few generic Christian "salvation type" phrases; finally, they urge viewers to "make a decision or commitment to Jesus Christ." Since this approach is almost the "standard in the industry" of Protestant evangelism approaches, it is no wonder a gentleman from Virginia recently wrote the Counseling offices of "The Lutheran Hour" saying, "I greatly appreciate your radio program . . . you explain the Gospel from a different standpoint than I usually hear."

As stunning as it may seem, "of the 176 religious program producers, agencies, and television stations approached by Horsfield in 1981, only six indicated they had undertaken independent research into their program audience for program effectiveness.[52] In addition, of those who have conducted independent research, most are reluctant to make the information public.[53] It is suspected by some that if it were revealed how certain elements of the electric church actually function, public support would quickly fade.

In order to determine how effective religious media is for evangelism, a number of research projects have been completed over the years[54]—however, comparing the various media outreach approaches is like comparing apples and oranges. Most of these research projects were carried out for quite different reasons. Therefore, it is difficult to say what research "over the past 30 years" has shown regarding "the effectiveness" of media-evangelism. At best, we can reach and only make general observations, and the conclusions we shall state can be only "qualified" ones at best.

One project, which drew great interest took place in Tallahassee, Florida, in 1974. It was undertaken to study the effectiveness of the approach used by the Christian and Missionry Alliance denomination in using media for the establishment of two new congregations. The mass communication employed was: (1) a five-minute daily radio program on one of the local radio stations, along with occasional spots; (2) weekly newspaper ads in the church page for special occasions; (3) television spots inviting people to attend the churches; (4) highway signs; (5) direct mail—to those people who move to or within the city.

The results of this media campaign indicated that at the end of the 18 months project, 40 percent of the general population and 82 percent of those who had attended one of the churches had heard of the sponsoring denomination; the main source of acquaintance for those in the church sample and general population sample was direct mail, which was named in 72 percent of the cases. Friends were the second major source, named in 25 percent of the cases; the television ads were named by only 5 percent of the respondents.

But even more important, when those who had attended the church were asked what the reason was for their attendance, 86 percent of the respondents said they had attended because of a personal invitation. The second most important reason—the newspaper ads—was named by only 8 percent of the respondents. None of those who attended said they were motivated to attend because of the television ad.[55] Now, let's be quite candid: since this was an isolated situation, further studies are needed. [56] It is also important to point out that these findings do not necessarily concern the majority of the evangelical/fundamentalist media "evangelizers" because they are not interested in planting local congregations, but rather they concentrate on building a TV congregation.

In our attempt to locate reliable research which would provide at least some indication of the effectiveness of media-evangelism, we cannot fail to mention the highly publicized 1984 Annenberg-Gallup Report. In a rare act of cooperation, the two prestigious institutions were joined by other TV evangelists and mainline churches.[57] As a result, this unprecedented and extensive project provided unlimited data and highly controversial conclusions; the most volatile was that: "although the evangelists raise their funds to reach the lost, they mostly reinforce people already committed to the evangelical religion."[58] Or, to put it simply: For evangelism purposes, media-religion is of little or no value.

Dr. John Bachman, a Lutheran clergyman (of the old ALC) and media-consultant was extremely provoked by these conclusions. In an insightful article which appeared in *National Religious Broadcasters* magazine, he pointed out that the "media mentality math" used to evaluate secular programs must never be used to evaluate religious programs; this is especially true, he said, if the evangelism "outreach potential" is to be determined. Bachman states: "Almost overlooked in the debate over media math is the fact that the regular audience should be of less interest than casual tuners-in. Occasional viewers may present the most significant opportunity for media contact."[59]

This then sharpens the focus of our study: if indeed one of the prime objectives of a religious media program is to interest the unchurched who happen to tune in, the total size of the viewing audience (made up also of many believers) is inconsequential. Or, if only a million viewers happened to tune in on a special carried by a non-religious station, the potential for evangelism would be much more significant for evangelism than the 20 million regular "religious" watchers. (Here again we must note that evangelical preachers striving to build a "radio congregation" will certainly disagree with this, since their primary goal is to build a radio or television "congregation" rather than to seek the lost in order to "fold them into" the local congregation.)

Now the hard questions: Given variety of research done on media-evangelism, what conclusions can be reached regarding its effectiveness?

"How effective is media-evangelism for carrying out the mission of the church?" Asking such a question would be similar to asking a visitor from Europe how "effective" he thought American Protestant churches were. His inevitable rejoinder would be: "Which ones?" Thus, practical examples are needed to explain why this question is unanswerable with a single statement.

For example, The Assembly of God Church in Los Angeles, with a 4,000 seating capacity worship center, and filled to capacity each Sunday, would be judged by most Americans as "very successful." Looking at the same church, however, a bishop in the United Methodist Church in Detroit might consider it "full of emotion and commotion," yet, being relatively "ineffective" because the church has no social programs impacting the surrounding community.

Likewise, a large United Presbyterian Church in a Chicago suburb with only 24 percent of its 3,000 members worshiping each Sunday but carrying on an extensive and high-level social program might be considered "extremely effective" by the executive secretary of the National Council of Churches; yet, this same church, when evaluated by the head of missions for the Southern Baptist convention, might be considered approaching the spiritual deadness of one of the ailing seven churches of the Book of Revelation.

Thus, we can see the difficulty of asking a similar question regarding media: "How effective is religious media for evangelism?" First, one would have to ask "Which program?" and then, "According to whose standards?" In attempting to obtain at least a minimal reading of the effectiveness of media-evangelism, three major approaches to media-evangelism shall now be presented. A description of how each group determines its effectiveness will be noted, and observations from their critics will be added.

The first "type" of media-evangelism would be that activity represented by the loosely knit group of evangelical/fundamentalists who presently constitute the majority of what is today popularly known as the "electronic church." This would include most independent evangelistic movements and also those having denominational connections. This is also the group whose primary goal (if not by intent—then by default) is to develop a radio or television congregation: a regular following who tune in and provide financial support.

At this point leaders of this group, or at least the acknowledged "Dean" of this movement, Dr. Armstrong, would say that they are doing well: the total number of viewers is well into the millions, prophecy is being fulfilled, and we can look for even greater things soon! Of course, the number of actual viewers of the "electronic church" has always been a source of controversy: at one time the *Wall Street Journal* estimated the audience of the "electronic church" at 128 million;[60] the prestigious Annenberg-Gallup report stunned a few people by its estimate of 13.3 million. [61] Pat Robertson followed the Annenberg-Gallup survey with his own survey (he commissioned the A.C. Nielsen Co. to measure the viewing audience again) and concluded that 61 million Armerican households were watching.[62] Yet, Dr. Armstrong might be closest in his estimate when he says the television viewing audience is most likely figuring in the neighborhood of 14 million.[63]

At any rate, leaders of the electronic church movement generally agree things are looking good; since they are primarily building viewer congregations and not looking for prospects for the local church, they would say their mission via the electronic media is "effective."

On the other hand, critics of the first group not only dispute the size of the listening audience, but they charge that research shows that few, if any, new members are being added to the church;[64] evangelical/fundamentalists are making no social impact [65] (which in the liberal mind is the chief task of the church); the success theology of the evangelical/fundamentalists plays into the hands of greedy network conglomerates.[67]

The second major category or group involved in media-evangelism would be those churches and groups who see the primary task of the church as that of improving society.[68] Interestingly, those who represent this point of view openly admit, though somewhat bitterly at times, that they are not nearly as "effective" as they should be. However, instead of seeing their lack of zeal or their over-obvious liberal theology as a major contributing factor, they rest the responsibility of their sad lot on the more recent rulings of the FCC[69] and the failure of Protestant churches to unite in an ecumenical effort to air joint programs of such a nature that even the greediness of the networks now embracing the fundamentalists would themselves be challenged and forced to change.[70] Thus, a simple summary of the effectiveness of liberal churches today regarding media-evangelism would be: Open acknowledgement by themselves of present failures and frustration.

The shrillest critics of the liberal attempt to use radio and television to improve society come from the fundamentalist/evangelical movement. These critics merely state that the failure of the liberal attempt is a direct result of their failure to "preach the Word of God;" therefore, people are not attracted to the programs and, consequently, they also do not support them.[71]

The unique Roman Catholic approach to media-evangelism is covered in a separate section of this paper. Therefore, the final category group attempting to use media-evangelism for evangelistic purposes would be those groups which use media as an important tool for locating evangelism prospects. The Lutheran Church is the largest group in this category. And, because of its doctrine of the church and because of its strong Bible-based belief that Christians need to gather regularly in a public assembly[72] in order also to receive the life-giving (efficacious) Word regularly through the Sacrament, Lutherans would not generally be considered part of the popular "electric church." Instead of building radio or television "congregations," Lutherans use the media as a "bridge device" to get people "interested in" and eventually "members of" a Lutheran congregation.

In media-evangelism, "The Lutheran Hour" was a pioneer. With the urgent voice and aggressive leadership of Dr. Walter A. Maier, "The Lutheran Hour," begun in October, 1930, realized its largest listening audience in the late 1940s when *Time* magazine reported a listenership of 12 million.[73]

After 20 years major changes took place: Dr. Maier died. Without a doubt, Dr. Maier's death in 1950 had a phenomenal impact on the broadcast. The entire field of media, however, was also shifting; television was emerging.

To take advantage of this new technological tool, the Lutheran TV program "This is the Life" was launched. Still running today, "This is the Life" experienced tremendous popularity in the '50s and the '60s. Again however, uncontrolled outside influences dictated changes. The Sunday morning TV hours which were initially available gratis to anyone with a quality program, now became a financial gold mine; competition became fierce; programs like "This is the Life" were forced into low-audience rated time slots. Other Lutheran attempts at television evangelism have been made by the Lutheran Church in America and the

American Lutheran Church.[74]

Lutheran Television of the LCMS has sought to regain influence through prime time specials. During the 1987-88 Christmas season, a one-hour, $1.2 million special, "The Little Troll Prince," is scheduled to be aired; promotional material suggests the results of the endeavor will be closely monitored. The results should assist in defining the future of Lutheran attempts in television evangelism.

This, of course, brings us to a most timely subject. With the advent of the celebrity television evangelists and all their claims to success, what has happened to "radio-evangelism?"

In the 1971-72 winter issue of *Journal of Broadcasting,* an article appeared with a most provocative title: "Who Listens to Religious Radio Anymore?" The data, gathered by author Ronald L. Johnstone in cooperation with the National Opinion Research Center, was an integral part of a national survey conducted in 1970 by the Lutheran Council of the United States concerning the image of Lutheranism. Several of the salient points were the following:

1. ". . . nearly half of the United States' (48 percent) adult population listens to a religious radio program at least occasionally. . ."

2. The 1970 results were "strikingly similar to a 1957 Casmir study; this led Johnstone to conclude at that time that 'no great change in proportions of persons listening to religious radio programs has taken place since 1957.'"

3. Those who listen also go to church and "there is relatively little contact with the uninitiated and the minimally committed." [Here, for purposes of this paper, "relatively little" deserves close attention.][75]

4. Regarding specifically "The Lutheran Hour," 48 percent of the total U.S. population had heard of the program; 20 percent listened at least occasionally; (this is a key finding for the potential effectiveness of religious media broadcasting for evangelism) and the survey showed that Lutheran Hour radio broadcasts were "reaching beyond the Lutheran denomination."

5. Eight percent of those who listen "hardly ever or never tune in." [Here again, for purposes of this paper, this seemingly insignificant statistic is absolutely crucial to the

entire presentation.]

6. In Johnstone's opinion, instead of an evangelistic tool, "religious radio programs serve primarily as a reinforcement function."

7. Two quite unexpected items surfaced. First, people in the southern Bible belt have consistently been heavy listeners of religious radio broadcasts. But this is reversed for "The Lutheran Hour" probably because a "church service type format is used and distinctively Lutheran, instead of Gospel, music is played." The second surprise is even more interesting: listeners of radio-evangelism are typically the older, female, and less educated. Lutheran Hour listeners, however, indicate there is no significant difference related to age; and "The Lutheran Hour" tends to pick up listeners who are more educated.

Thus, while research data on the current effectiveness of Gospel broadcasting on radio and television is quite limited, the studies available indicate a surprising number of people who hear religious programming regularly and also a significant number of "occasional" or "accidental" listeners are always tuned in. The potential for evangelism must not be overlooked.

In the most recent detailed annual survey of Lutheran Hour listener mail, 17,972 pieces of mail were received in the Counseling Department. (It is estimated that nearly again as much mail arrives with only a financial contribution and is processed by the Data Entry Department.) The majority of non-financial contributing listeners requested items offered on the broadcasts. The most requested item was "The Lutheran Hour" calendar, followed by the Advent devotional booklet. Fifteen percent of those who wrote in received a pastoral reply; and 61.3 percent of this same group wrote in because they had a severe problem.

In the same year, the Counseling Department received 14,267 letters as a result of the television broadcast "This is the Life;" jewelry was the most requested item sought by 41.2 percent of inquirers to "This is the Life," followed by books, 25.4 percent, and Scripture portions by 15.5 percent.

In this same 12 months, 6,855 names of Lutheran Hour listeners were sent to area pastors for possible evangelism follow-up;

7,654 individuals who had written in to "This is the Life" were also referred to area churches. The International Lutheran Laymen's League also airs additional programs such as "Crosswalk" and television "specials."

The potential for church membership as a result of using religious media for locating prospects can be seen from the following letter received in the Counseling Department:

"I've been listening to your excellent radio program. I have also begun attending a Missouri Synod Church in this area. I would like to know more about the beliefs of the Missouri Synod Lutheran Church . . . I have already told friends about your inspiring radio program."

Now, let's take a brief look at the "imaging power" of television in regard to electronic evangelism. This also will permit us to glance at the use of the media for evangelism by the Roman Catholic Church. Historically, Protestants in the United States have been wary regarding the Roman Catholic Church and especially the Papacy. This negative image has correspondingly been a constant burden for the Roman Catholic Church in its efforts to "fold in" or evangelize more converts: primarily those who do not now attend church but who possess residual Protestant attitudes.

In the last decade, there has been a change—and this change can only be described as "astounding;" following the Pope's 1979 widely televised U.S. tour, the Gallup poll survey revealed that by May of 1980, an amazing 89 percent of all people interviewed in the United States had a "favorable" opinion of the Pope.[76]

Even more amazing is the fact that by 1980, teens across the United States selected the Pope as the "man they most admired," even ahead of the United States President.[77]

For purposes of further understanding, let us ask the question: "Are the Pope, the Vatican public relations officials, and the Congregation for the Propagation of the Faith unaware of the use of 'images'?" By no means! They not only take advantage of those which occur naturally; but many of the images they are involved in, they themselves create and then capitalize on.

Irrelevant as it may sound to some, let us keep in mind that the Pope himself is a disciple of the Dale Carnegie course, "How to Win Friends and Influence People." [78] He studied acting as a college student, traveled as part of a theater group and hoped to become a professional actor;[79] he knows well how to communicate the image of the Holy Father as a pious, white-haired leader having no ulterior motives whatsoever toward Protestantism, and only serving as a "pilgrim for peace."[80]

Thus, we need to discuss created "images" as a counterpoint to reality. Along these lines, the *New York Times* has a number of times emphatically pointed out the television camera which is permanently mounted in the Holy Father's popemobile.[81] This "eye" to the public is constantly focused on the Pontiff making it possible for a complimentary image of the Pope, and, with him, the Roman Catholic Church, to be immediately available to all networks during his national tours. Thus, even though his critics may be many, as much as possible, the head of the Roman Catholic Church is shown in a positive light. Indeed, who would argue with the *New York Times,* which observed that: "according to television experts, the Pope knows exactly what he is doing when confronted with a camera."[82]

According to Edward L. Hirsch, senior field producer for ABC news and a veteran of a half dozen Papal trips: "He clearly understands television . . ."[83] Which also caused Rome bureau chief Wilton Winn to add: "John Paul II, has a real knack for getting into the news."[84]

And, of course, the Pope is not unaware of the image versus reality game. "Major U.S. newspapers are received [at the Vatican] by mail and read daily, along with about 30 others from Italy and the rest of the world. Articles are clipped, summarized, and translated into Italian each morning . . . although the original text is included, too. The Pope and top Vatican officials receive a copy of the digest—which can be as long as 20 pages—around mid-morning. Usually the Pontiff tries to read it . . . but can finish it only in the evening—due to visitors. In addition, the group prepares a twice monthly review of international background articles that are 'both favorable and unfavorable' to the church, the official said."[85]

Although the Vatican has only recently been able to utilize the "evangelizing" potential of television, the Roman Church has long understood the tremendous power of images to promote its cause. *Maclean's* magazine of Canada (a sister to *Time* magazine of the United States) in its "Art" section, observed that, "Propaganda, now a pejorative word, was once synonymous with art dedicated to high purpose. It was used in the campaign of the Roman Catholic Church in the 17th century to propagate its teachings and counter the challenge of Protestantism.[86] It enlisted the finest artists and artisans of the day in a massive public relations campaign." Amazing, isn't it, to see how the tool the Roman Catholic Church used already 300 years ago to propagate its faith and to thwart Protestantism has now gone its full course and is being implemented in an even more effective way through television? Here, again, we see that the Roman Catholic Church is more prone to use images than to state its teachings clearly in propositional truth.

Instead of trying to evaluate the intention of the Roman Catholic Church in its public relations/evangelistic use of the media, it might be better to listen to columnist Dick Dowd of the official Roman Catholic newspaper, *The St. Louis Review,* February 22, 1985. Dowd writes: "A lot of printer's ink has been given to these questions [as to the value of the Pope's foreign trips] over the years. The Canadian bishops seem to be the first to find a measurable answer. They commissioned a Gallup poll of all Canadians . . . just a year after the Pope [visited]."

And what is the value of a Papal visit? According to Dowd: "The obvious advantages are significant, sometimes overlooked." Three out of four of those who saw the Pope on TV felt an emotional involvement, especially when watching the Pope's meeting with the sick and handicapped or young children. One out of three went so far as to count themselves changed by the Pope's visit. They felt a renewed faith, according to Dowd.[87]

Realizing the impact and benefits the Roman Catholic Church receives from a major Papal tour, it is not difficult to understand why the Roman Catholic Church encourages rather than discourages all the hoopla and imaging that takes place when the Pope moves around the world and creates even what certainly sounds like blasphemous hysteria.[88] How ironic then to read that the Pope turned to 400 reporters who were covering him and in a public relations gesture, told them: "You are indeed servants of the truth."[89]

For casual observers of the U.S. electronic church, the use the

Roman Catholic Church has made of television may appear to be quite insignificant—especially in comparison to the high profile of Jerry Falwell, Jimmy Swaggart, and Robert Schuller. But, for those behind the scenes and pulling the strings, it is truly as one Catholic editor stated: "In this sense, the Papal trips are examples of powerful, full-court media-evangelization **unmatched by anything in history.**"[90]

The Roman Catholic faith, as it is generally presented to the public and even to the faithful, in its liturgics and images is so filled with ritual and mystery that, in order to make maximum use of the stunning power of television it has, instead of employing weekly programs such as Falwell and Schuller, resorted to major blitz appearances to the public. These well-planned, financed, and calculated barrages tend to propagandize and visually mesmerize the viewers by their sheer awesomeness and excitement. And what does it all mean? One *Newsweek* journalist said: "[After all is said and done] the viewers have no knowledge of what the Pope really represents."[91]

Is it then only the large and powerful Roman Catholic Church that specializes in 'imaging' through the media? By no means. According to the *New York Times,* Thursday, September 19, 1985, ". . . for the last eight years or so [the Mormon Church] has also been attempting to change its image with the general American public by running public service spots under its name that promote moral conduct. The 'family' is usually stressed. It is a kind of advertising that is intended to get the viewer to think: 'Their values are the same as my values, so they have to be okay.'"[92] The *Reader's Digest,* by the way, has also carried these attractive ads.

How effective has the Mormon campaign been nationwide? Amazingly so! In fact, so much so that when the prestigious New York advertising firm of Ogilvey and Mather wanted to put some new power into their firm, they turned to a most unusual place: they went to Salt Lake City young people (four of the five are Mormons), and gave them key positions in their firms.[93] The company bosses realized that these young people knew exactly what they were doing. They had proven that, through the use of television, images speak loudly, and propositional truth often has very little to say.

While this may be somewhat dismaying, it also raises a challenge to Christian writers, pastors, and professors. Deceptive imaging provided by religious media can be effectively combatted by the printed page. The West German publisher Hubert Burda, whose company has annual sales of $1/2 billion, recently explained: "TV creates a whirlpool of images that swirl about in people's minds that need to be calmed and interpreted. That is the big opportunity of the print and media."[94]

Now, having glanced momentarily at a most interesting use of "television imaging" primarily by the Roman Catholic church and the Mormons, let us return again to the general discussion of using media for evangelism. We have seen some of the innate deficiencies of the media in evangelism; we have witnessed some of the abuses. Yet, considering all the negative elements, let us state loudly and clearly that in spite of all criticism, apologists and critics still agree: **the unchurched do tune in.**[95] And so we finally arrive at the crux of the question: Is the number who accidentally or inadvertently tune in "significant" enough to merit the money spent to underwrite the media program? This then leads to the inevitable subject of cost effectiveness.

In discussing the "cost effectiveness" issue of media-evangelism for our particular purposes we might get to the real issue quite quickly in a practical (though hypothetical) way by suggesting the following scenario. The International Lutheran Laymen's League administers "The Lutheran Hour," and "Lutheran Television," plus related ministries with an annual budget of approximately $14 million. By expending this amount of money each year, 'X' number of members are added to Lutheran congregations worldwide. Now, if the same amount of money, $14 million, were instead used to build a seminary, the question would be: "Would the graduates 'evangelize' more 'unsaved' in the world than is being accomplished presently through the media efforts?" It's great, of course, to say that both are needed—but any practical man knows that sometimes both may not be possible. Of course, one might also argue that the radio/TV broadcasts also "nurture" and "reinforce" those who are already Christian; but for this situation this particular argument is irrelevant if, in the first place, the $14 million is solicited in order to evangelize the unsaved. This is not a suggestion; rather, it is a hypothetical scenario for purposes of understanding the issues.

Finally, let us also never fail to point out that, in spite of all the criticism of the electric church, the number of inquiries received for counseling as reported by various evangelistic groups is simply impressive! Broadcasts which offer help to viewers appear to be especially effective in attracting a large phone and mail response.

For instance, after a five-day nationally broadcast crusade from Philadelphia in 1960, the Billy Graham association received over 600,000 letters in a five-day period. In 1978, it received more than one million letters from its radio and television audience. The "Old Time Gospel Hour" in 1978 received an average of 10,000 letters each working day and the Oral Roberts organization receives such a volume of mail that it has established a mail room with a handling capacity of 20,000 letters a day.[96] In analyzing the evangelistic potential of these inquiries one would need to determine whether a "freebie" or "give away" was offered instead of literature or counseling material, since this is the key for analyzing evangelistic potential in any phone or mail response.

Some involved in media-evangelism feel that better contact is possible when the program provides opportunities for telephone contact; and many of the paid-time religious broadcasters now have this facility. . . . The PTL Network claims that in 1979, "more than 478,000 calls were received on these 'prayer lines.'"

The amazingly large numbers of inquirers can be interpreted in many ways; yet, even the harshest critics must admit that, if candidates for evangelism are honestly being sought, such an outpouring of resonse must contain at least a goodly number of "candidates" for the Kingdom. This is especially true when the opportunity for spiritual counseling is offered instead of religious jewelry and other freebie gimmicks.[97]

Along these same lines, while some may find the following story extremely humorous, it nevertheless did happen, and the results should blow "a powerful lot of wind" into the sails of those who seek to use the media as a tool for locating evangelism prospects.

In early 1982, actor Ned Beatty was portrayed as an evangelist on ABC's Monday night movie. The "spoof" show was called "Pray TV" and it included a fake "800" number for viewers to call in to receive counseling and help. The producers were astounded at the results. An estimated 15,000 people tried to dial the phony number, seeking help for their problems in life.[98]

Thus, from many perspectives it can be shown that the media is an extremely useful tool for locating evangelism prospects; sadly, therefore, the questionable image painted by some critics of media-evangelism still seems to cause a number of parties previously interested in using this tool of technology for locating the lost to curtail or even terminate their interest; this need not be so! Excesses in media-evangelism have obviously been committed by some; poor theology[99] (and even no theology)[100] has been the hallmark of others.[101] In addition, liberal critics claim that more social-oriented programming is needed if the Christian church is to accomplish its task in society. Are these the only alternatives? Absolutely not!

The Key to it All: The Living Word

God has given us unlimited evangelistic power through His living Word. Speaking through Isaiah the prophet God says that His "Word," when it is proclaimed, shall not return until it has "accomplished" that which He desires. The efficacy of God's Word is explained by the revered Biblical scholar Delitzsch: "[The Word] is not a mere sound or letter. As it goes forth out of the mouth of God it acquires shape, and in this shape is hidden a divine life, because of its divine origin; and so it runs, with life from God, endowed with divine power, supplied with divine commissions, like a swift messenger through nature and the world of man, there to melt ice as it were, and to heal and to save."[102]

In other parts of the Scripture we see that the Word is more than (as is often seen in Protestantism) mere authoritative sound sent forth to trigger man's potential. Contrary to popular opinion, no man has spiritual potential[103]—no man has a free will in matters of faith.[104] This Word alone can establish life where there is none;[105] it is a living and dynamic agent;[106] the efficacious Word removes vain religion and plants saving faith.[107] It is only the Word and neither our power nor our pious desires which cleanses[108] and sanctifies[109] us in the true faith.

A clear understanding of the Biblical doctrine of the Word is absolutely essential to an effective approach to evangelism and missions. Embracing the now popular Protestant understanding of the Word of God automatically leads one to constantly seek new methodologies in order to evangelize or carry out a mission program. Interestingly, when Paul in his loving admonition to Timothy gave the simple and yet all-embracing command and approach to missions, "Preach the Word," this apostle was imparting an inspired message which the bulk of today's media-religionists apparently do not comprehend.

Thus, we agree with Luther that the Word does not merely trip man's trigger of potential . . . for natural man has no spiritual potential (Eph. 2:1). Instead, the Word affects even that which it commands—it not only calls for conversion and sanctification, the Word itself converts and sanctifies.

The Word is efficacious. A serious study of Luther's introductory sermons on the Gospel of John would be a stunning surprise to many involved in today's "electronic church." His approach to the Word, totally different from what is held by the majority of evangelicals today, yet, solidly Biblical, is indeed exciting; in fact, it is so inspiring, it is so energizing, that if this understanding of the Word were recaptured today by Protestants, there would be a new Reformation, and a phenomenal mission and evangelism threat, even among Lutherans!

This sin-cleansing and life-giving Word not only can be sent out effectively over the air waves; indeed, it must be urgently proclaimed via this medium as we seek every avenue to find the lost sheep, working while it is day before the night comes when no man shall work.

And . . in all our media-evangelism activities, Let the examples of Jesus be our guide.

In this presentation we have repeatedly cited statistics; statistics assist us in our kingdom work; yet, they must never become our master. This is especially true when we are tempted to compromise the Christology or theology of aired programs so as to draw the greatest audience.

When these temptations occur, let Jesus' clear example be our guide. In Mark, chapter 1, we read where Jesus spoke and exorcised a man on the Sabbath morning. Later that day He miraculously healed Peter's mother-in-law; that evening He healed and exorcised many more; finally, He retired.

Early the next morning, while He was still praying, Peter came searching for Jesus. As he found the Savior he said excitedly: "Everybody is looking for you." (As if Jesus did not know this.) We can also hear Peter saying: "O Jesus, the Nielsen ratings are up, you are a celebrity—let's ride this wave of popularity all the way into Jerusalem/New York. You will be the greatest media star in history."

But alas, how Peter's dream must have been dashed when Jesus, fully aware of the crowd potential, turned instead the other way, and said, "Let us go somewhere else to the towns nearby, ... that I may preach there also; for that is what I came out for."[110] In brief, Jesus was not interested in those who followed Him because they sought signs, wonders, or entertainment. He was interested only in the proclamation of the Word. Thus, we must conclude: no matter how successful the program, no matter how large the audience, if the Word is not preached, all the activity is useless.

Two additional examples from Jesus are also crucial for this presentation. Matthew 9:36 tells us that, as Jesus looked out at the crowds who followed Him, he saw them as "harassed and helpless," starving spiritually—being led by legalists and religionists—but having no true Shepherd to lead them and to feed them.[111]

Amazingly, the spiritual state of our affluent and techno-logically-oriented society is no different.[112] If anything, our generation's spiritual condition is worse. Realizing the desperate spiritual state of many of us should move us to labor diligently in the Kingdom and use every tool at our disposal, including the media. Knowing the terrible end of the unsaved should move us to encourage all men to embrace Jesus by faith, to live in Him, to cling tightly to Him, and to nourish themselves daily on Him and His Word.

In addition to the impoverished spiritual state of millions even in our own land, the astounding following of Shirley MacLaine and the New Age Movement[113] should urge us on to point all who will listen to the gracious offer of Jesus, "If any man is hungry, . . . let him come to me . . . I am the Bread of Life."[114] And, "If any man is thirsty let him come to Me and drink."[115]

This new life is found neither in increased religiosity as regularly measured by the Gallup poll,[116] nor in the anti-Christian Lodge movement; it is found neither in the "inactive" church membership;[117] nor in any of those who practice religious self-righteousness. New and true life comes only when one is grafted into Jesus Christ through the power of the Word in Holy Baptism.[118] To receive Jesus Christ means to be baptized into Him and His death and then to rejoice each day over the full assurance of His total pardon from the curse of our sins.

All this comes through the preaching of the cross; to some this is foolishness—but to those who believe, it is the power of God unto salvation![119] Thus, in our media outreach the message can never sway one iota from the clarion call of Paul: "We preach Jesus Christ and Him crucified."[120]

It is often said that the Gospel of Mark reads like a newspaper: there is constant conflict and crisis. Indeed, this is so; and the root cause of this conflict was the teaching among the people by the Pharisees that acts of religiosity, no matter how vain, were required for salvation. The Pharisees did not originate this; they only measurably reinforced the most powerful religious conviction in man.[121] This certainly is true also today in much of our society.

Thus, in our media presentations we are not called to act as mere smiling PR representatives, reflecting the current grotesque stereotype of a benignly smiling Jesus; but instead, since we speak for Christ,[122] and as we face the damning power of self-righteousness worldwide, we must hear the call of Jeremiah as our own: I have appointed you this day over nations and over kingdoms, to pluck up and to break down, with the living Word of God to destroy and to overthrow all who trust whatsoever in self-righteousness and "to build and to plant" through the power of the Word, the Gospel.[123]

And so, for the final example of what we can learn from Jesus as we use media for evangelism, we turn to Alfred Edersheim. It is no accident that this brilliant historian has devoted one full chapter of his monumental work, *The Life and Times of Jesus*

The Messiah[124] to the call of Matthew.[125] In Matthew's day the Pharisees obfuscated the numerous Gospel promises of the Old Testament; as a result, virtually no one could qualify in God's sight but they themselves.

Matthew was an experienced man of the world; moreover, we can confidently assume he was also well versed in Jewish religion; but according to all religious standards of the day as set forth by the Pharisees, Matthew was not only a sinner—but one of the very worst kind.[126] Consequently, there was very little spiritual hope for this tax collector.

Thus, when Jesus began preaching on the shores of Galilee within ear shot of Matthew's tax collecting booth, this Jewish civil servant, employed by the Romans, began to hear a new message; and he could not believe his ears!

According to Jesus, salvation was by grace and not by works; therefore, surprise of surprises, even Matthew could qualify! This was like a breath of fresh air to a man being very violently strangled by legalism.

Thanks to the zealous work of today's holiness preachers, many on television, our society teems with those who feel the way Matthew did.[127] Either by personal failure or by their lot in life, they are convinced that if there is any hope whatsoever, God will have mercy on those who "do their best."

Thus, we need to use every tool at our disposal, including the media, to reach those being spiritually strangled by the damnable cause of popular religiosity, to proclaim liberty to the captives of legalism, and to announce freedom from the supreme anxiety of life's end to all who live in the prison of the fear of death.[128]

Conclusion

The subject of the "electronic church" and the question of whether the electronic media can be "effectively" used to reach the unsaved is a complex one, indeed. The "Christian" church of today is comprised of a variety of theologies; as a result, these diverse and sometimes opposing theologies precipitate a variety of approaches for carrying out the mission of the church.

Thus, when one inquires as to the "effectiveness" of the electronic church, one must stipulate precisely which of the many evangelistic programs is being evaluated and also the criteria used. As previously explained, an approach used and considered successful by one group may be considered ineffective or even harmful by another.

The evangelical/fundamentalists who presently comprise the bulk of the most popular religious media programs, especially on television, would consider their own efforts as quite successful and even as the fulfillment of prophecy.

Spokesmen of the more liberal church bodies are highly critical of the use of the air waves by fundamentalists and evangelicals. They are also frustrated in their inability to produce widely acceptable ecumenical types of programs; and they are further frustrated in the failure of the general public to support programming they deem beneficial toward the change and improvement of society.

Of the three major categories or groups using media for evangelism (there are other minority parties not covered in this paper), the final one is represented primarily by the Lutherans. The approach used by the Lutherans is also the most difficult; yet, it remains the most Bible-based since it bases nothing on man and everything on God and His Word.

Lutherans support neither the idea of creating a "radio pulpit" nor a "television congregation." And because of their distinctive understanding of the Word, Lutherans see the primary goal of religious media, not as a device for creating radio or TV "congregations," but rather as a tool for locating lost sheep, and returning them to the fold. There they can receive life and nourishment through public worship, public preaching of the living Word, and reception of the life-giving Sacraments.

It is total folly to argue that the religious media, (radio or television), is unable to get people to respond and to make inquiries through phone or by letter. Numerous examples can be shown to demonstrate that the media cannot only elicit these responses, but that the media can trigger an almost incredible response. But the crucial element still remains: what type of response does the inquirer receive and how is the inquirer handled? Two additional related challenges are: can the inquirer be brought all the way into the fellowship of Christ and be catechized; and finally, will the inquirers be able to joyfully gather each week with other believers to hear the living Word and to receive the life-giving Sacraments?

Indeed, in order to accomplish this, the implementors of media-evangelism face the great challenge of getting people who respond to a radio and television program to take the next step; that is, to continue their inquiry as to precisely who Jesus is, how to receive a saving relationship with Him and how to worship Him regularly and become part of the Body of Christ which meets each week for nourishment from the living Word.[129]

Since there is overwhelming evidence that phenomenal responses can, indeed, be generated by media-evangelistic programs, and since the next step, which is so crucial, especially in the Lutheran approach, is that of transferring prospects into church membership, the approach taken once the initial inquiry reaches the mail Counseling Department is absolutely critical.

Just sending a letter of religious encouragement is inadequate. The Gallup poll constantly reveals that the bulk of the United States population knows and uses many Christian "buzz" words. Yet, these inquirers lack a comprehension of the basic salvation doctrines. Therefore, it would seem absolutely incredible that any media-evangelism approach could be operated without regularly offering a Bible study correspondence course. The type of doctrine offered in most media programs is, by the very nature of media-religion, going to be somewhat generic and watered down; therefore, it is necessary to get evangelism prospects into the Word and teachings of Christ as soon as possible. In addition to the offer of the Bible study correspondence course, a most prayerful approach must be used for each inquiry so that even the slightest indication of interest might be translated into a strong and vigorous thirst for the Gospel; and again, this is accomplished only through the efficacy of the Word.

Lutherans, therefore, have selected the most difficult method for employing the media for evangelism. On the other hand, seeing the Word as efficacious, Lutherans go forth in their task knowing that nothing depends on man; but everything depends on God; He has promised that His Word, when proclaimed shall not return void—It shall not return until It has "accomplished" that for which It is sent. No greater promise is available on the face of the earth. Let us therefore go forth with boldness and confidence.

1. Malcolm Muggeridge, *Christ In the Media* (Eerdmans, 1977) p. 33 ff.

2. Muggeridge casts a jaundiced eye at television because he says, by its very nature, television conveys fantasy instead of truth. He is not alone in his criticism. Situations have also occurred in radio where speakers have resigned because they decided, as a matter of religious conviction, that the proper preaching of the Word of God cannot be done on radio. As he left his work on the Mennonite Hour, speaker David Shank wrote to the governing board. He admitted "he did not know how to please the listener (to get him to turn on the program regularly and **not** off) and yet, tell the listener what he doesn't want to hear: the prophetic Word. . . ." [Shank concluded that the "Gospel radio broadcasting in the USA is basically a form of pampering—and essentially a prostitution of the Word."] *Mennonite Broadcasts—The First 25 Years,* (Mennonite Broadcasts, Inc., 1979) pp. 52-53.

3. Ben Armstrong, *The Electric Church* (Thomas Nelson Publishers, 1979) p. 7.

4. According to the [1987] *Directory of Religious Broadcasting,* a publication of the National Religious Broadcasters, edited by Ben Armstrong, 1,061 religious television programs and films are available for use in the United States; in the same year 807 radio programs were aired; 282 organizations were producing religious radio/television for use outside the United States; 414 organizations produced television programs for domestic consumption; 596 produced religious radio programs for domestic use; in 1987, 221 religious television stations were in operation (an increase of 11 percent over 1986); in 1987 a total of 1,370 radio stations were in operation—a 21 percent increase over 1986.

5. George Gallup and George O'Connell, *Who Do Americans Say That I Am?* (Philadelphia: Westminster Press) p. 22.

6. William F. Fore, *Television and Religion* (Augsburg, 1987) p. 77.

7. Many questioned whether the sacred Word of God could be proclaimed through the use of an electronic machine. One official of the Anglican Church was especially bothered because men might now be able to listen to the Gospel "with their hat on."

8. Virginia Stem Owens says: "Theologically (a radio church) is a contradiction in terms." Owens, *The Total Image,* pp. 63-64.

9. A Detroit pastor, using a special local channel, claims he ministers to his flock effectively via TV. "Why bring people out miles and miles . . . when they can get the message in their own living room?" *Detroit Free Press,* November 11, 1981.

10. Consultant Sam Sherard, using examples of local congregations which employ television to broadcast their services, claims that "a church with attendance of 1,000 can minister effectively to 40,000 over the air." Sam Sherard, "Media Expert Says TV Helps Build Church Attendance," *Religious Broadcasting,* January, 1977, p. 39.

11. This has always been the understanding of the Confessional Lutheran Church as reiterated by Holsten Fagerberg, citing Article VII of the Augsburg Confession: "The church is the assembly of saints in which the Gospel is taught purely and the sacraments are administered rightly." Holsten Fagerberg, *A New Look At The Lutheran Confessions* (Concordia Publishing House: 1982), p. 251.

12. This is openly evidence by Rex Humbard's annual television communion service "inviting all believers who are watching at home to participate while gathered around their television sets." (See Armstrong, p. 84) Also Kenneth Copeland's World TV communion service in 1982 drew an estimated 600,000 people and was viewed live by satellite teleconference in over 200 U.S. cities and in 17 foreign locations.

13. When examining the many works published on media evangelism, virtually all parties, critics, and apologists cite Armstrong freely, thus conceding that Armstrong is perhaps the best spokesman for the "electronic church."

14. Armstrong, p. 8.

15. Ibid., p. 9.

16. Ibid., p. 9.

17. Ibid., p. 10.

18. Ibid., p. 10.

19. It is also admitted by the author that "some" (apparently a minority) were reluctant to accept this new concept.

20. Armstrong, p. 172.

21. The evangelist/politician Pat Robertson at the dedication of a special CBN earth station in Virginia Beach, Virginia, said: "The most exciting 'line feed' came from Jerusalem where some singers standing right outside the eastern gates sang 'Even so, come Lord Jesus.' That brought tears to my eyes," Robertson said, "because we were looking at the place where He is going to come back." The Bible says: "Every eye shall see Him" *and we were looking right where it was supposed to happen.* Ibid., p. 170.

22. Ibid., p. 173.

23. Ibid., p. 173.

24. Besides using the electronic media to "reach the unsaved," and to establish a "more complete (?)" understanding of the "church," some evangelicals also see control of the media by "born again" Christians as a way to improve television and society. In an editorial in *Religious Broadcasting,* Harold Hostetler writes: "As Christians, we need to pray both for network takeovers and for the conversion of those now in control of the networks." *Religious Broadcasting* (editorial), June, 1985, p. 40.

25. *Washington Journalism Review,* April, 1986, p. 40.

26. In a letter to the editor of *Time* magazine, a lady from Kansas wrote: "Pat Robertson is more valuable as a Gospel preacher than as a candidate for political office. He should stay right where he is. I have read more books as a result of watching the 700 Club than I ever read after listening to sermons in the Lutheran Church. *Time,* March 10, 1986, p. 26.

27. A brief sampling of recent letters received at "The Lutheran Hour" counseling offices include: Oceanside, California: "The hour is 7 a.m. . . . I accidentally tuned in The Lutheran Hour . . . at [the age of] 86, if you're smart . . . you talk to God a lot;" Monett, Missouri: "My husband and I are 'team' truck drivers, and we travel coast to coast. On July 19th, we heard The Lutheran Hour over the PA at the Rip Griffin truck stop in Moriarty, New Mexico, while having

breakfast . . . ;" Woodbridge, Virginia: "You explained the Gospel from a different standpoint than I usually hear. I would like to receive more information . . . ;" Ridgeway, South Carolina: "[Your program] has helped me to know more about Christ and His love and kindness . . . ;" Kingston, New York: " . . . Your program gives me great strength;" Sydney, Ohio: "While driving in my car this morning, I happened to hear your program. . . . Please send me a program schedule. . . ; Monterey Park, California: "What a great sense of peace and contentment I felt after hearing your program . . . ;" Dennison, Iowa: "Please send us a copy [of the sermon] as we would like to send it to a missionary friend in Africa;" Houston, Texas: "Divorce, and absolute disaster in my life 15 years ago—a continuing disaster and heartbreak even now. Thank you for your comforting message;" From prison (Menard, Illinois), an inmate wrote: "I know the cockroaches will be out again tonight, crawling, sniffing, feeling the hairs on my legs, as I try to sleep. . . . The decision of the court is so final . . . 50 years for attempted murder . . . 50 years for rape . . . my psychologist doesn't give a damn (is it too late for me?) . . . does anybody care?" San Rafael, California: "I am in search of God as a reality. . . ."

28. Extensive articles have also appeared in major secular magazines such as *Time* and *Newsweek.* In addition, *TV Guide* has carried special featurs on the electronic church. On occasion, secular journalists do point out significant areas of concern they foster regarding "Christian" media activities. However, for the most part, we are not interested in these evaluations due to the extremely liberal and anti-Christian bias inherent in the secular press. Issuing a statement that the media/press is extremely liberal frequently causes considerable reaction. However, before "flying off the handle" on the basis of emotion, it would be especially beneficial to examine: S. Robert Lichter and Stanley Rothman, "Media and Business Elite," *Public Opinion,* October/November, 1981, pp. 42-46, 59-60; and Linda Lichter, S. Robert Lichter, and Stanley Rothman, "The Once and Future Journalist," *Washington Journalism Review,* December, 1982, pp. 26-27.

29. For example, William Fore (often quoted in major news publications such as the *New York Times, The Christian Science Monitor,* and *U.S.A. Today*) sees the increased use of television by evangelicals and fundamentalists as primarily a historical and sociological phenomenon; **but not necessarily theological;** that is, they do not necessarily use media as a result of their desire to take the Great Commission seriously. Fore sees the popularity of evangelical/fundamentalist media zeal as a response to the upheaval of the radical '60s: they thus appeal to their listeners to bring back the stable "good old times." William F. Fore, *Television and Religion,* (Augsburg Publishing, 1987) pp. 74-77, 88.

30. In a *U.S. News & World Report* article entitled, "The Mainline Churches Strike back," the author concludes with this sentence: "Even so most media experts agree that, because television is so pervasive, major denominations have a *duty* to see that their views get on the air." *U.S. News & World Report,* February 15, 1982, p. 60.

31. In this endeavor, some churches have tried a bit of cleverness. For instance, one of their ads states: "Did Jesus Christ survive crucifixion only to be nailed by the Nielsen ratings?" Another showing a baptismal font states: "There is a

difference between being baptized and being brainwashed." *UM Communicator,* October, 1981, p. 6.

32. "In the process they [electronic church broadcasters] may have done considerable damage. . . ." Horsfield, p. 166.

33. *Wall Street Journal,* November 21, 1985, p. 33.

34. Even Dr. Ben Armstrong, the primary target of much of Horsfield's scathing criticism, gave a very positive endorsement of Horsfield's work. The endorsement which appears on the back cover of the book says: *"Religious Television* by Peter Horsfield is a very well-researched book and represents the best treatment of this subject in recent years."

35. Dr. Fore is a Methodist minister with a divinity degree from Yale and a Columbia Ph.D. His latest book. *Television & Religion* has just been released by Augsburg Press, Minneapolis. *Christian Science Monitor,* July 22, 1987, p. 21.

36. Horsfield, p. 145.

37. Ibid., p. 147.

38. Ibid., p. 44.

39. Armstrong gives examples of local congregations which dramatically increased their membership by televising their services locally. Armstrong, p. 163.

40. Horsfield, p. 150.

41. Ibid., p. 142.

42. Furthermore, since my religious media programs tend toward "religious" PR than solid doctrine, the opportunity for the viewer to more seriously consider the critical doctrines of the faith is seldom offered.

43. For example, a frustrated Lutheran, bored with what he would consider unexciting liturgics might prefer to worship in front of a "stage" rather than an altar as he watches Jimmy Swaggart "croon," backed up by a set of drums, guitars, base, etc. Keeping in mind the weakness of the flesh, few people would dispute the fact that it is common sense that most "religious" people would prefer an "entertainment" approach over a liturgical worship service.

44. Horsfield, p. 146.

45. Armstrong says people change churches because previous ones did not preach the Word of God. Armstrong, pp. 151-152.

46. "Evangelicals: Out of the Closet But Going Nowhere?", Carl F. Henry, *Christianity Today,* January 1980, p. 16 ff.

47. *U.S. News & World Report,* April 23, 1984, p. 68.

48. This temptation is not peculiar to religious television. NBC News anchor Tom Brokaw admitted: "It's tricky trying to generate understanding and insight while not ignoring the entertainment factor." *Newsweek,* July 13, 1987, p. 13.

49. George Comstock, *Television and Human Behavior* (New York: Columbia University Press, 1978), p. 172.

50. Interestingly, along these same lines there is now a Christian television program in the Philippines which sponsors the Philippine Charity Sweepstakes where home viewers may participate in a grand raffle.

51. Ibid., p. 39.

52. Ibid., p. 82.

53. *Religious Television,* preface, p. XV.

54. Horsfield gives a listing of the major research projects conducted over the

years, briefly describing each. This helpful listing available in his book is too extensive to include in this paper. He also explains that most of these reports differ in their goal; thus, it is, also, in his opinion, impossible to answer the question of how effective religious media is for evangelism. Horsfield, p. 83 ff.

55. Ibid., p. 143.

56. The results of this project appear extremely dramatic in a most negative way towards media-evangelism. Thus, since this is only one isolated instance, it would be questionable as to how much credence this research should receive among those interested in missions and outreach . . . at least until further probing is done. At any rate, the results were exceptionally interesting and should at least provide a start for further exploration.

57. The project was a "two-year study commissioned by a coalition of 39 religious agencies, conducted by the Annenberg School of Communication at the University of Pennsylvania and the Gallup organization, and completed in 1984." John W. Bachman, *Wasteland or Wonderland* (Augsburg, 1984 0 p. 75. An astute criticism by Bachman also appeared in the May, 1985, issue of *Religious Broadcasting*, p. 22.

58. *Time*, Feb. 17, 1986, p. 62.

59. *National Religious Broadcasters* Magazine, May, 1985, p. 22.

60. *Wall Street Journal*, July 11, 1980.

61. Fore, p. 103.

62. Ibid., p. 104.

63. *Religious Broadcasting*, "Facts About National Broadcasters," February 19, 1978.

64. "Evangelism, in the sense of reaching out to find and convert people not already reached is ineffective. . . ." Fore, p. 109.

65. Horsfield, p. 160.

66. Ibid., p. 22.

67. Ibid., p. 158.

68. This then explains why Horsfield, definitely of the more liberal theological bent, draws on such liberal theologians as Paul Tillich to interpret the theology needed for effective Gospel work via the media. Ibid., p. 39.

69. Ibid., p. 9.

70. Ibid., p. 180.

71. Armstrong, pp. 151-152.

72. Hebrews 10:25.

73. *Time*, October 18, 1943.

74. J.W. Bachman in his essay "Second Thoughts on Annenberg" makes reference to such attempts along with results. *Religious Broadcasting*, May, 1985, p. 22.

75. Here again, the total number of regular listeners to the program is not nearly as important as the number of those who accidentally tune-in or hear the program because it was on a station already being listened to. This element is extremely crucial and we must refer once again to Dr. Bachman's astute analysis of the Annenberg-Gallup report; this sheds important light on the Johnstone report.

76. *Emerging Trends*, Princeton Religion Research Center, vol. 2, no. 6, June, 1980.

77. Ibid., vol. 2, no. 5, May, 1980.
78. *Quad-City Times,* August 31, 1986.
79. *U.S. News and World Report,* June 27, 1983.
80. However, his point rating of personal peity might drop quite quickly when it is learned that he can be quite "salty" in his personal comments. Ibid., p. 20.
81. *New York Times,* September 17, 1984.
82. Ibid.
83. Ibid., September, 1984.
84. *Time,* February 4, 1985.
85. *St. Louis Review,* August 9, 1985.
86. *Maclean's* March 17, 1986.
87. *St. Louis Review,* February 22, 1985.
88. During his trip to one foreign country, the local people began to chant: "He is light."
89. *Newsweek,* October 15, 1979.
90. *St. Louis Review,* February 22, 1985, p. 13.
91. *Newsweek,* October 15, 1979, p. 95.
92. *New York Times,* September 19, 1985.
93. Ibid.
94. *World Press Review,* September, 1987, p. 59.
95. Eight percent of listeners to "The Lutheran Hour" radio broadcast "hardly ever or never attend church." Ronald Johnstone, *Journal of Broadcasting,* "Who Listens To Religious Radio Broadcasts Anymore?," p. 91; even in a listening audience of one million, (8 percent or 80,000) would be a phenomenal sized audience of evangelism prospects. Here again we must read closely the astute analysis of the Annenberg-Gallup research report by Dr. Bachman. Regarding evangelistic potential of media religion, his following comments deserve serious attention:

    1. He correctly dismisses the endless argument (often taken up by the secular media regarding **total** audience size) especially in its comparison and its potential, since we are primarily interested in the occasional "tuners-in." "Almost overlooked in the debate over media math is the fact that **regular audience should be of less interest** than casual tuners-in. Occasional viewers may present the most significant opportunity for media contact."

    2. "An audience which may be small for commercial television may be . . . significant in lost sheep mathematics."

    3. "A lost sheep approach would note the significance of the finding that three percent of the viewers disclaim Christian or Jewish ties. Broadcasting is such a pervasive medium that crumbs falling from the network cables may represent far more outsiders than are reached by any other method undertaken by the church. The typical congregation does not attract many unchurched to regular worship services. Even a few hundred media contacts present an opportunity." Second thoughts on Annenberg, *Religious Broadcasting,* May, 1985, p. 22.
96. Horsfield, p. 139-140.
97. The questions of the ethics involved in soliciting listener responses by

offering jewelry and other gimmicks is quite serious. It is generally understood in the religious media industry that offering "Christian" jewelry and other freebies is a gimmick borrowed directly from the secular world of high-powered business. Horsfield notes, page 30, that when a person sends away for a free gift, "he or she is more prone to be responsive to a request for a contribution;" thus, the entire procedure goes hand in glove since the **primary reason** the jewelry and other freebies were offered to begin with was to get people tied in to a fund-raising mailing list. Thus, all individuals involved in media-religion must use extreme caution since God surely will not honor those methods which are in any way deceptive. Horsfield even goes so far as to correctly observe that certain money-raising procedures "represent a modern return to the purchasing of indulgences. . . ." Horsfield, pp. 30, 34.

98. *Detroit Free Press,* Feb. 4, 1982.

99. Covering Robert Schuller in its "Religion" section under "Apostle of Sunny Thought," the editor of *Time* magazine notes that Schuller's critics "complain about his message . . . that he is mass marketing ersatz, individual-centered Gospel that glosses over the troublesome doctrine of sin." The article further states that "Religious history books will be talking about Schuller 100 years from now," but the question, according to historian Dennis Voskuil, "is whether [Schuller] will be remembered as a theologian or a showman!" *Time,* March 18, 1985, p. 70.

Also, anyone interested in an honest appraisal of Schuller's theology should certainly obtain a copy of the tract by Richard P. Belcher entitled, "The Impossibility Thinking of Robert Schuller." Belcher, a Baptist pastor, was also, at one time, a student at Concordia Seminary, St. Louis.

100. *Newsweek* noted: "As a self-made preacher, [Jimmy] Swaggart has little formal theological training . . . St. Augustine, he claims, . . . came up with doctrines which have caused millions to be lost." *Newsweek,* May 30, 1983, p. 89.

101. One of the "great" media preachers, Norman Vincent Peale, in a moment of honest reflection admitted: "So many of my sermons didn't amount to much." Considering all preachers will stand before the judgment throne to answer for their handling of the Word, that is a frightening self-indictment. But it is more understandable after hearing Peale also confess, "My job is to reach them all . . . I try to talk about what is basic in Catholicism, Protestantism, and Judaism: love, fellowship, esteem for human beings—they all understood that." *Parade* Magazine, May 17, 1987, p. 5.

102. Keil/Delitzsch, *Commentary On the Old Testament,* vol. 7, p. 359. Luther also speaks of the Word as an active agent in his sermon on John 1:1-7; St. Paul also speaks about the Word being "at work" within believers (2 Thess. 2:13).

103. Luther's exhaustive work *The Bondage of the Will* is a thorough treatment of man's helpless spiritual condition as stated in the Scriptures. For those interested in a shorter and quite provocative treatment, they might turn to the April, 1966, issue of the *Concordia Theological Monthly,* p. 207. This article, "Luther Against Erasmus" was originally delivered by James I. Packer the well-known Anglican author and clergyman to the pastoral conference of the English Lutheran Church, October 30, 1964.

104. Ephesians 2:1; Colossians 1:21; Colossians 2:13; Romans 9:16; John 1:13.

105. John 6:63.

106. *Luther's Works,* American Edition, vol. 22, p. 13.

107. Jeremiah 1:9, 10; Romans 10:17.

108. John 15:3.

109. John 6:27.

110. Mark 1:38.

111. Matthew 9:36.

112. In an extensive cover story entitled "Happiness—How America Pursues It," *U.S. News and World Report,* in a 12 page "special report" outlined the myriad of ways people today attempt to find peace, meaning, and happiness in life. The article is interesting. **But the conclusion must have come as a shock** to most readers when the author wrote: "Yet Americans, despite polls showing that some 90 percent claim to be 'happy,' never quite get their fill." *U.S. News and World Report,* March 4, 1985, p. 60 ff.

113. The "New Age" movement is a sub-culture that combines elements of a 1960 style distrust of conventional institutions with a bevy of mystical philosophies. *U.S. News and World Report,* February 9, 1987, p. 68; an estimated 25,000 "New Age"—oriented bookshops now operate in the United States; the September 9, 1986, issue of the *New York Times* notes: "Representatives of some of the nation's largest corporations, including IBM, AT&T, and General Motors, met in New Mexico last July to discuss how metaphysics, the occult and Hindu mysticism might help executives compete in the world market place. These are strands in a thread of alternative thoughts that scholars say are working their way into the nation's culture, religions, social, economic, and political thought.

114. John 6:27.

115. John 7:37.

116. Regularly, the Gallup survey indicates that well over 90 percent of all Americans "believe in a God."

117. Some rather dubious concepts of Christianity have been surfacing of late. The August 30, 1987, issue of the *Minneapolis Star and Tribune,* following a statewide religious survey reported that "Minnesotans have a far deeper religious faith than such common measures as church membership and attendance might indicate. They overwhelmingly believe there is a God who watches over humankind in response to prayer. But these beliefs don't always result in going to church, praying, or reading the Bible."

118. Romans 6:4.

119. 1 Corinthians 1:18.

120. 1 Corinthians 1:23.

121. Romans 2:14.

122. 2 Corinthians 5:20.

123. Jeremiah 1:9-10.

124. A. Edersheim, *The Life and Times of Jesus The Messiah,* 1 vol. ed. (Grand Rapids: W.B. Eerdmans, 1971).

125. Edersheim, Chapter XVII.

126. And Matthew was one who, according to Edersheim, belonged to a "class, to

whom, we are told, repentance offered special difficulties."

127. "The Lutheran Hour" counseling office receives countless letters regularly from people who say: "I love Jesus; I believe in Jesus; I trust and have faith in Him—but I am not a Christian;" this torturous cry of despair is a result of holiness preaching: exhorting people to get their lives straightened up so that they can then be prepared to receive Jesus and be saved.

128. Hebrews 2:15.

129. No area is more crucial in Lutheran media-evangelism than the "step": getting the inquirer (no matter how finite their interest might be) to continue this interest in making a Spiritual inquiry. In this, next to the "preaching" itself, the most important "department" in a media-evangelism organization is the Counseling Department. Here again, clearing away the communication barriers so that the spirit of God can work is only done through the proclamation of the living Word.

ROBERT D. PREUS, Ph.D., D. Theol.

Dr. Preus has been president of Concordia Theological Seminary, Springfield and Ft. Wayne since 1976. He received a B. A. from Luther College, Decorah, Iowa in 1944, a B. D. from Bethany Lutheran Seminary, Mankato, Minnesota in 1947, a Ph. D. from Edinburgh University, Scotland in 1952 and a D. Theol. from Strasbourg University, France in 1969. He has also studied at Harvard University and in Oslo, Norway. He has served as pastor in Mayville, North Dakota, Cambridge, Mass. and at several locations in Minnesota. In addition to his administrative duties, he is recognized as a scholar in the areas of Lutheran Confessions and seventeenth century Lutheranism. He is the author of *The Inspiration of Scripture, The Theology of Post-Reformation Lutheranism,* and *Getting Into the Theology of Concord,* along with many essays and articles. He lives in Ft. Wayne with his wife Donna. They have ten children.

LUTHER THE COMMUNICATOR

Robert D. Preus, Ph. D., D.Theol.

I am very flattered and honored to be able to speak to you this morning on the subject "Luther as a Christian or Evangelical Communicator". I don't see myself as particularly qualified for this; I am no authority on communications, nor am I a Luther scholar, but perhaps there is no one in the world who is an authority on both of these at the same time. So, perhaps I can bring a few things to your attention that may help us to understand Luther better, but more importantly, to understand the tremendous contribution he made to history and also to us as we attempt to communicate the Gospel today.

But before we get to the subject of Luther, I would like to say a few words about communication, even though other speakers have discussed this topic with more thoroughness than I wish to do.

First of all, what is communication? I want to start with a definition of the word, a generic definition of what communication is. The word "communicate" means "to share;" it means to impart, to transmit something to someone so that the other person or party shares in what we transmit. In a sense, it means to give someone something, yet at the same time still to retain what you have given him. Now, that generic definition of communication should be followed by a little description of what communication is. What's the nature of communication? That's very simple, I believe. You have a communicator, the one who communicates, and you have a communicant, if I may use that word, the one to whom something is communicated. And the third element is—that which is communicated. And the result of this communication is very often what we call "communion", that is—two people, or two parties, now have something in common. And that's called "communion," "fellowship," "unity," "commonality," and many words like that.

Now, I would like to say a few words about types of communication—what is communicated? I think that you can classify communication into four types. First, there is a **communication of attributes.** Those of us who are pastors and theologians know this, because of our doctrine of Christology. We talk about the "communicatio idiomaticum." This is a term that was used by the old Greek fathers and by the Latin fathers and by our Lutherans. It refers to the fact that the two natures of Christ are in communion with each other, but the divine nature communicates to the human nature of Christ divine attributes such as omnipotence, omnipresence, omniscience, and so forth. So that Jesus Christ, God and man, has divine attributes, also according to His human nature. But you can have a genetic communication of attributes, too. I have blue eyes, my wife's eyes aren't quite so blue, but somehow we communicated blue eyes to all ten of our children. You could have communication of something bad, a disease, the plague, AIDS. So there are all kinds of what we might call ontological communication or communication of attributes.

Secondly, we could talk about **aesthetic communication.** That's the kind of communication you have in art or music. We think of men like Michelangelo in his day, a painter; Renoir, in his day, an impressionist painter; Picasso, in our day. The point is that they communicated to a lot of people; that is artistic communication. Or music: Wagner, in his day; Bach, in his day; Prince today—I haven't really heard him, but most people seem to like him.

Third is emotive or **affective communication.** If you were with me out in the mountains of Glacier National Park last summer, you would have been walking along and all there would have been was a picture of a grisly bear. That picture communicated fear and emotion, and it communicated them very well. Another example: dread. You may have seen the movie about the holocaust in Cambodia called *The Killing Fields.* You didn't have to see a thing or hear a thing, just watch the actor walking across those bodies that communicated the nature of a holocaust. Or you could communicate something like joy or happiness. The best communicator in our country, at least according to the standards of many, is Bill Cosby. I read in *Forbes Magazine* that he made $84,000,000 in the last two years. He makes more than any executive, any entertainer, any boxer; nobody makes as much money as he does in this country. And what is he communicating, in his own homelike way? Just a feeling of happiness, joy; he makes people laugh, and he is very successful. I have a daughter in Evanston; her name is Ruth. She is the happiest, most pleasant girl I've ever met in my life, except of course for my wife. That's what you call genetic communication. The minute she walks into a room, she communicates joy, optimism, happiness. And it's not only to me, but she communicates that feeling to everybody.

There is a fourth kind of communication, and that's what we're talking about today, though the first three are united with it. And it is called **cognitive communication**; that's what you've been hearing about mostly. And it has a very broad base. This type of communication takes place at the universities and the schools. Math textbooks communicate mathematics to math students, and so forth. Out at the Air Force Academy, they communicate certain knowledge and skills that are didactic, cognitive in nature, so that the students will learn how to fly airplanes and so defend our country. The *Wall Street Journal* communicates news about the stock market; the sports section of your daily paper tells you the scores of the games. St. Louis just won the pennant last night, and so forth. Now, the Scriptures are first among cognitive modes of communication. Never forget that.

The next thing I want to talk about by way of introduction are the **ingredients of effective communication**. Once again, I want to say that these are my ideas. I haven't read them from any text books, but as I see it, there are four basic ingredients of effective communication. I'm speaking generically now, about communication in general. First, you have to identify your audience. For instance, at Purdue, engineering students would be the audience of a professor in the school of engineering. He is not interested in those who are taking English—or other courses. He has a specific, identifiable audience. It's the same, for instance, in other cases. I'm sure Bill Cosby's audience is the entire United States of America, anybody who watches TV or watches his movies or reads his books. Our whole culture practically—at least the English speaking part of it—is his audience. The same might be said for Ronald Reagan, the President of the United States. In the case of John Paul II, who has just been here, his audience would be two-fold. First of all, Roman Catholics in this country. But if you see his excellent communicative skills, it will be the entire country. He's a real public relations artist. Karl Marx sat in London most of his life, writing silly books, but he knew who his audience was. It was the whole world, just as the pope's is. So the first ingredient is to know who your audience is.

Secondly, you need understanding and insight into your audience. You have to know something about the audience, the communicants, as it were. I would submit once again that our good friend Bill Cosby or Franklin Roosevelt or John Paul II are all master communicators in terms of knowing their audience. John Paul knew exactly what he was going to come up against in this country, and he dealt with it very effectively from his point-of-view. He communicated. Third is an understanding or insight into what you're willing and wishing to communicate. If you are teaching mathematics at Purdue, you'd better know lots of mathematics and understand your subject matter as well as you possibly can. That is the first basic requisite of a good teacher and a good communicator. The same is true with flight skills at the Air Force Academy or with any ideology, such as Marxism or Christianity or Buddhism, or anything else—you have got to know what you are communicating. You must understand it fully.

Fourth is that more vague ingredient that I call ability, skill, or gift to communicate effectively. And that's hard to define and it's hard to inculcate in a person. But it happens, and again I would simply mention men like Cosby, John Paul II, Renoir, and maybe even my daughter Ruth. But men like Hitler or Goebbels were also effective communicators because of an ability and skill they had to get their message across, evil as it might have been.

Our speakers have also talked about **theological communication**, and so today I would just like to give you a few basic principles.

First, as we talk about the communication of the Gospel, or theological communication, I want to say this. Theology and the

Gospel are first of all, cognitive, informative discourse about God. That's the nature of theology. Secondly, the source and norm of all theology, of all our communication of the Gospel, is the Scriptures. **Sola Scriptura**—only the Scriptures, God's Word, his communication to mankind. We have heard plenty about that already. Third, the audience of God's communication, which our speakers have talked about a great deal. It is the entire world, including all cultures, all nations, all strata of society, all age groups, excluding no one, absolutely no one. Fourth, the means of communicating theology and the Gospel is teaching. "Teaching them to observe all things whatsoever I have commanded you." "Go ye therefore into all the world and preach the Gospel to every creature." That Gospel is a didactic, cognitive message; it is taught. Now I am talking about teaching in a very broad sense, using every possible context: preaching, witnessing, liturgy, *seelsorge,* pastoral care, comforting and helping people, Bible classes, catechetics, and so on.

Fifth, in communicating the Gospel by teaching, the communicator will employ all technology, art forms, and emotive devices compatible with the message that he wants to communicate. Now that's a very loaded statement, and every word counts, so I will repeat it. **In communicating the Gospel, by teaching, informing people, the communicator will employ all technology, art forms, emotive devices compatible with the message that he wants to communicate.** I have a son who is a pastor, and he said, perhaps three or four years ago, "Is it possible for a Lutheran to communicate effectively and according to Lutheran principles by using TV?" His problem was you couldn't celebrate the Lord's Supper, there was not tactile brother-to-brother, personal relationship, just a person sitting there looking at this boob-tube. Can you communicate effectively that way, where there is no congregation present? Aren't there a lot of factors lost? All I could say was that we have to communicate. We better—unless it is not compatible with the Gospel, and, of course, TV is a perfectly neutral tool. So we must use it. Our problem is that we haven't quite found out how to do it effectively.

Next point: The greatest communicator of God's Word, or of the Gospel, is God himself. Dr. Voelz made that very clear yesterday. But why do we say that? Because God knows his message perfectly; he knows all theology. He knows perfectly his audience, this fallen world of ours. And he knows perfectly how to communicate. We speak about the perfection of the Scripture. It is totally clear and sufficient to bring people to a knowledge of the truth and to save them.

Then the Church and the Christian communicator, you and I, will imitate Christ as best we can in today's society, in today's context and culture. And we will imitate the Scriptures, which is his word to us today. So, with that bit of lengthy introduction, let's get to Luther.

I believe, and I am sure there are many people who would agree with me, that Luther is one of the most effective communicators in all history. And he is the best communicator of the Gospel and of Christian theology since Apostolic times. I say that because he has grasped the message, the content of his communication, better than almost anyone else since the Apostle Paul. He knew his audience, and he used all the means of communication available to him. Those are the kinds of things I'm going to be talking about, Luther as a Christian communicator.

First of all—as an educator. Luther was called to the University of Wittenberg, where he became a professor of exegesis. There wasn't much exegesis back in those days; people were communicating through commentaries on St. Thomas Aquinas, and it was a more dogmatic, philosophical presentation of the Christian faith. And it was almost totally ineffective. It didn't reach the people. Luther saw if you were going to reach the people, you had to reach the pastors, and if you were going to reach the pastors, you had to reach them with the Scriptures, and so he was an exegete. And during his lifetime, that's what he valued the most of all his activities. He produced a number of commentaries, most of which were not written, but just taken down in notes, I believe. Those commentaries abide with us today. I am thinking of his commentary on Genesis. It is quite a few volumes in the American edition, perhaps six or seven. And perhaps an even more significant commentary is the one on Galatians—in two volumes. I would say that every pastor here and every layman here could buy those books and get tremendous benefit out of them. He communicates in those books, but we need to know why. It was because he knew the original languages.

He knew the message of those books, and so he communicates their message very effectively, so much so that I daresay no other commentary on Genesis and no other commentary on Galatians has sold as many copies, even up to today. I know Professor Buls uses Luther's commentary in his Galatians course, and I use it in one of mine that isn't even on exegesis. That's how well Luther communicated as an exegete, as a professor of exegesis.

Secondly, Luther communicated as a catechist. He wrote the Small Catechism in 1529. I suppose at that time there were fifty catechisms circulating around Europe, a good many of them were in Latin, but some of them were in the various vernacular languages. These didn't catch on, while Luther's did. His work totally obliterated the field, except in Roman Catholic countries, where it wasn't allowed. Even when the Reformed came on the scene, they used Luther's catechism because it was such a good teaching device. It was the Scripture, the layman's Bible. Now, why was it so good? Basically, it starts with the evangelical content at the center. Luther centers on the work of God, and on Christ, as Creator, Redeemer, Sanctifier; he clusters everything else around that. Secondly, Luther writes to an audience that he apparently understands very well—children. It's memorizable. Some of you and I have memorized it. That means it can be memorized as a summary of the Christian faith, a type of what Paul says to Timothy, "Hold fast the pattern of sound words which you have been taught," and so forth. This is a pattern of sound words that even a child can manage. I still quote the catechism. I maintain that there is nothing taught at the Seminary that can't be assessed by the catechism. This means that every layman who knows the catechism can pretty well judge his pastor.

It's good for another reason. Germans, you know, write in long sentences, and when you translate them, you have to break them down into about three American sentences. Interestingly enough, the sentences in the catechism are long, though I don't think Luther spoke in long sentences. Why are they long? Because he wants to incorporate in one sentence the entire content of a topic that he is touching upon, whether it is the explanation of a certain commandment or a petition or even those long sentences in the creed: I believe that God has made me, I believe that Jesus

Christ, and so forth. Here is one case where a long sentence works, because even a child can understand it and memorize it. Organization, balance—everything is there.

Continuing on the subject of Luther as an educator, I would like to remind you that he didn't just teach at the university; he was a teacher to the Church at large. He wrote treatises on such subjects as Christian liberty, the Babylonian captivity of the Church, and a long treatise on the bondage of the will, original sin, and human degeneration since the Fall. These books became immensely popular, and people read them because they communicated. Luther wrote in Latin because he wanted pastors to read them and other people who could read Latin in those days. And they came out in paperback. Here is a case where Luther, I think, leads the way. Printing was invented about fifty years before he was born, but it was mostly the Bible and Aristotle, Plato and some of the classical authors that were translated. The popularity of tracts and pamphlets began with Luther. They were cheap and they could be printed quickly, and printers everywhere under the sun pirated them, because they had no copyright. And so the word that got out was written in a very compelling, simple, almost rustic Latin form, pretty much German put into Latin. And it communicated all over the Western world. Luther perceived the level of his audience in every case. If he was writing to the theologians, you knew it. If he was writing to the Papists, you knew that, too. And if he was writing to the Lutherans, that also was obvious. If he was writing to an overall group of people, especially lay people, he wrote in German, which hardly anybody did in those days. Educated people thought they were too good to write in German. Erasmus and the other great humanists wrote only in Latin; in fact, they were so good they wrote in Greek, a language that nobody understood, I guess, except other Greek professors. You can't communicate that way. Luther spoke German, and he spoke the German of the people. Just plain, blunt, simple language; it wasn't coarser than any other. It was just the way people spoke, and that's the way you communicate. It's also the way you communicate theology. So Luther perceived the level of his audience in every case.

Second, how did Luther communicate as a hymn writer? He was the one who introduced hymns as an integral part of worship.

He communicated every aspect of religion in his hymns, the didactic side, the aesthetic side, the emotional side; he put everything into his hymns. He wrote these hymns because people didn't sing very many hymns in those days. But hymns became an integral part of worship almost immediately and also a part of the life of the people. Later, hymn books were the devotional books of the Lutheran people. They didn't need a Book of Common Prayer like the one the Anglicans had. The Lutherans had their hymnbook. In my opinion, it's kind of a sad thing that hymnbooks are getting heavier and heavier every generation. You just can't put them into your pocket the way we used to do and ride a streetcar or a bus or an airplane and sit and read the hymnbook. I used to do it, but no more—the big, bulky things. Now they have to write out the music for us; they didn't have to do that back in those days.

Another point about hymns is their aesthetic and emotive elements. These are not cognitive in themselves, but are very closely related to the culture of the day. Luther used these elements effectively. He used familiar, singable tunes, and he adapted the tune to the words. In the case of "A Mighty Fortress is Our God", the tune serves the words. And in the case of "Lord, keep us steadfast in thy Word" I want you to hear it the way it originally was, the way I learned it as a child: "Lord, keep us in Thy Word and work,/Restrain the murderous Pope and Turk,/who fain would cast from off His throne,/Christ Jesus, Thy beloved Son." That's what the German says, and it communicated, believe you me. We're not communicating today with hymns. Luther did, and the tune helped.

Now, I want to say something about the use of rhyme. Not all hymns have rhyme, of course; sometimes they have meter. But rhyme facilitates the retention and memorization of a hymn. You know from your childhood how you used to sing the songs that were going around—tunes that had a melody that Helen Forest or Frank Sinatra or whoever it was sang, like Prince and similar entertainers today. At any rate, Luther rhymed his hymns. I maintain that you can learn something that's in rhyme and music four times as fast as you could learn a basic Bible passage or other piece of literature from the catechism. What this means is that you have at your disposal an instrument for memorization and retention, which today we have lost. I'll never forget when I was in Norway years ago with my wife and relatives; she had a cousin who had us in and who went around the house all day singing hymns in Norwegian. That's the way it used to be. That's what you can do with hymns to build up personal devotional life as well as add to public worship. Hymns unite people.

In Lutheran hymns, we find a blend of teaching and doxology. The old Latin hymns were all doxological, but they were didactic, too. Luther taught the message of the Gospel in his hymns. And they were hymns of praise, so while people were praising God and learning, they were being edified by the very content of the hymn.

Now I want to say something about the Christological/ soteriological content of the hymns, if I may use those words. The hymns were centered in Christ and His work of salvation. Read Luther's hymns; they are models in this respect, much better than most of the hymns that came after him. In their hymns, Methodists talk about how you feel. In our hymns, Luther talks about what God has done. And by telling what God has done, he created in his hymns the same emotive and aesthetic response that Wesley achieved.

Finally, Luther's hymns are Biblical. They are based on Biblical texts or Biblical themes or, like "Dear Christians, one and all rejoice," they summarize the whole Christian faith in one hymn.

Third, I want to say something about Luther's communication as a liturgist. To begin with, he simplified the formula of the mass, which was the usual service, by deleting all offensive and unevangelical elements. He made the service simpler. Then, too, he structured the service around the means of grace. The Word, preaching, became central, along with the Sacrament of the Altar. Also, baptism, too, may have been central, though we don't know about that. Next, he made the sacramental aspect of worship dominant, rather than the sacrificial. In other words, what God is doing in the service is more important than what we do. Not that we do nothing, not that we don't respond, praise God, pray, and so forth, but the important thing is that the Word is coming to us and edifying us and informing us and comforting us.

Luther also put the liturgy into the vernacular, German. It took the Roman Catholics 400 years to see the wisdom of that. Luther did it right away, the *Deutsche Messe,* which spread up into Norway and Denmark and all over the evangelical world. He brought worship elements into the catechism, like the *Te Deum,* and other aspects of worship so that the little children could learn worship forms and the theology of worship even at an early age, while they were preparing for more adult church worship.

In all Luther's liturgy, he proclaimed the cognitive, the kerygmatic, the proclamatory Gospel, without losing any of the doxological, emotive, and aesthetic elements of worship. And, finally, he avoided unnecessary changes. I don't think he would have been too enamored of our way of having a new, revised hymnbook and order of service every thirty years. I am not saying which hymnbook is best, you understand.

Next, a few words on Luther as a confessor. In this regard, I bring your attention to *The Smalcald Articles,* which are included among the Lutheran Confessions, overlooked today, but they are equal in clarity and organization to the *Augsburg Confessions.* They are as fine a summary and confession of faith as any written and they are deeply and commitedly evangelical.

Then, too, we should consider Luther's communication as a translator. Somebody should give a whole paper on this topic, but I would like to emphasize today that Luther knew the theological content of the Scriptures, and he also knew the original Biblical languages, Hebrew and Greek, from which he did his translating. Also, Luther knew his audience better than Jerome or any other translator. He knew his audience, and he knew their language and thought forms. This is why Luther's German Bible is probably the best translation in the history of all translations, because it communicated accurately to the people of his day.

To close, I'll refer to Luther's communication as a preacher. He brought preaching back into the service and into the life of the church. His sermons were always didactic; he preached expository sermons and also sermons on the chief parts of the catechism. He preached them at the level of all his audience, which was the entire church, and so we say that his sermons were eloquent in an earthly sense, but not in an ornate, classical, or baroque sense, which communicated only to a few. This way, Luther reached the widest audience possible.

Professor Bunkowske said a few years ago that the Reformation was more than a reformation: it was an evangelical movement. I say it was a great evangelical mission movement, and it was great because it communicated the Gospel better than any other movement and better than any other theologian has ever done, I believe, since the time of the apostle Paul. It will do us all well to know this and to imitate Luther whenever we can today. Thank you.

ROBERT D. NEWTON

Rev. Newton is a 1977 graduate of Concordia Theological Seminary, Ft. Wayne. He served as an evangelistic missionary to the Kankanaey people in the Philippines from 1978-83, where he ministered in a remote mountain area of northern Luzon, the largest island in the Philippine archipelago. During this time he was involved in planting new congregations and outstations along with training laymen to work as spiritual leaders. Since then he has been doing graduate study at the School of World Missions, Fuller Theological Seminary, Pasadena, California, and he has assisted the Southern California District in developing a cross-cultural leadership training program. He is currently instructor in missions at Concordia Theological Seminary, Ft. Wayne. Rev. Newton and his wife Priscilla have three children.

THAT THEY MAY HEAR

A sermon preached by Prof. Robert D. Newton
on October 1, 1987
Text: Romans 10:5-17

The formula seems so simple—Faith cometh by hearing, and hearing by the Word of Christ. And so it is. Those of us who have never been far from the Word of Christ, who received that Word in baptism during our first weeks of life outside the womb; those of us who grew up with the preaching of Christ week after week by faithful pastors and teachers and nourished on the Word in bread and wine; yes, those of us who have always had the Word near to us, in our hearts and on our lips, do we realize how simple it is— Faith cometh by hearing and hearing by the Word of Christ. It would do us all a great bit of good to live for a time among people who do not have such a simple life. Go to Nigeria, or Japan, or inner city Detroit, to downtown or uptown Ft. Wayne, or live for a week next door to Shirley MacLaine. If you want to experience complicated religion, go see how the other half lives, each looking for something or someone to believe in, each struggling to establish a righteousness of his own. Look in their eyes, see the desperation etched in their souls as they perform another animal sacrifice, chant another empty prayer, or seek out a more in-tuned channeler. Such profound ignorance! That they only knew how simple it is, Faith cometh by hearing, and hearing by the Word of Christ.

That they only knew! That was Paul's earnest desire as he by the Holy Spirit penned the words of our text read from the lectern a moment ago. I would now like to read the four verses that precede them:

> Brothers, my heart's desire and prayer to God for the Israelites is that they may be saved. For I can testify about

them that they are zealous for God, but their zeal is not based on knowledge. Since they did not know the righteousness that comes from God and sought to establish their own, they did not submit to God's righteousness. Christ is the end of the law so that there may be righteousness for everyone who believes.

Paul's concern conveys a two-pronged pathos which belongs to every man who claims to follow in the footsteps of the apostles—a burden for those who have heard the Word of God countless numbers of times and yet who struggle in unbelief, and those who are also numbered among those nonbelievers, but only because the Word has not yet drawn near to them. It has not been communicated to all peoples.

This missions congress has focussed on the topic of communication. By the time it ends, it will have addressed God's communication to His people of old through His appointed prophets. It will have spoken of these latter days when God's communication came in His Son. It will have spanned the centuries to give us insights as to how Luther and the other reformers proclaimed the Gospel to the world of their day. And it will have brought to our immediate attention the myriad needs of peoples all over the world to hear the precious news of salvation and the equally myriad opportunities God has provided through speech and sign, radio and printing press, at home and across seas, to the familiar and the exotic, to bring that Word near to the hearts and lips of the 3.5 billion yet without Christ in this world.

But for a few minutes this morning I would like the text to address you and me as communicators of God's Word and the particular ways his Word goes out from our midst to others. It centers in three verbs in the text, all dealing with speaking:

> to preach,
> to confess,
> to call.

I. To Preach

This word really means to herald. A herald is one who is officially sent out by his master with the commission to speak in the master's behalf. He is responsible to communicate exactly what his master has told him to say, because he is not speaking for himself, but for his master.

That is what Paul was saying in these words, "How shall they believe in him whom they did not hear." If people are to believe in Christ, they must hear Christ speaking it to them. This is the task of the herald.

And what they must hear of Christ is what He said of Himself. The Son of Man came not to be served but to serve and to lay His life down as a ransom for many. To be heralds we must speak this one thing—I preach Christ and Him crucified.

A herald is sent out. Paul goes on in the text, "How can they herald, unless they are commissioned?" An essential characteristic of a herald is that he is officially commissioned (given an assignment and the authority to complete it) and sent out.

This word is carefully used in the New Testament, and in every instance it refers to one officially sanctioned by Christ or His Church to go out in behalf of the Lord with the Gospel. This is what has come down to us today in the office of the public ministry—men officially commissioned by Christ through the Church to speak in His behalf to the nations. Christ has established this office; we do not have the right to abandon it.

Nor do we have the right to ignore its particular functions. It is not enough to say that a herald is one who officially speaks for Christ. He is, to be more precise, one who is sent out to speak for Christ. Being sent out is an essential element as well. A herald takes the master's message as far as there are people to whom the message is addressed. Our text clearly identifies the parameters of Christ's realm, His intended addressees, "the Lord is Lord of all."

That brings us back to a right understanding of the Word of Christ. It is a seeking Word. That is why Paul reminds us we are not to go looking for it—by ascending into heaven or descending into the abyss. Men cannot seek it out. It seeks them out and finds them. To be a herald, the office to which many of you aspire, means that you become a seeker for the souls of men.

II. To Confess

All are to confess Christ. While not all Christians are commissioned as public preachers of Christ, all are to confess Him. "If any man confesses me before men, Him will I confess before my Father in Heaven, but if any man denies me before men, him will I deny before my Father in Heaven."

Don't be turned away by these words. Understand that this confession springs from a heart of faith. And this faith is created by the Word which is preached.

What is the content of this confession? Jesus Christ is Lord. It embraces His death; it clings to His resurrection. It holds firm the fact that He is ruler over all the universe and will one day gather all things back under His graceful dominion. But, what does it mean to confess Jesus as Lord? That phrase is used a lot today, but one wonders if it is really understood. What does it mean to embrace and then confess Jesus Christ as Lord?

For that, let's turn to our last verb, "to call."

III. To call upon the name of the Lord

This is the oldest form of communicating the Word. It dates back to the earliest chapters of Genesis. It is the mark of the believer and is distinguished by this one characteristic—he daily comes before the throne of God, who is rich toward all who call upon Him, and there he confesses his need for mercy and grace. "God be merciful to me a sinner." This is the prayer of the one who calls upon the name of the Lord. And it is in this prayer that we most loudly confess that Jesus Christ is Lord.

The thief on the cross is one example. The Word was near to him, only a few feet away. He could see it; he could hear it as it pronounced absolution to the world. The thief saw his wretchedness, his utterly desperate condition, and he saw the Word's answer to his hopeless condition. In a moment the Word entered his heart and found its way to his lips, and he confessed that Jesus Christ is Lord by calling upon that name, "Jesus, remember me when you come into your kingdom."

We are called to communicate Christ. Through the public preaching of the Church, through our private and corporate confession and through our calling upon Him daily we speak to ourselves and the world that there is a God who is not afar off. He is near, and shall be forever. Amen.

PANEL DISCUSSION

Objective:
   To apply the Biblical theology of Scripture in identifying ways to communicate Christ in an increasingly technological era.

Question One:
   Communication in Biblical times was primarily done without technological media. What does the Biblical model have to say to us in terms of Gospel communication today?

Question Two:
   What impact does communication technology have upon cross-cultural ministry and missions at home and abroad?

Question Three:
   Communication is often limited by world-view differences between the culture, or sub-culture, of the hearer and the culture, or sub-culture, of the Gospel communicator. What needs to be done to make certain that God's intended message is actually communicated for understanding?

Question Four:
   What can local pastors and laymen do to carry out a more full communication of God's message in their local context of ministry?

Prof. Wenthe

I'd like to address the first question: communication in Biblical times, which was done primarily without technological media. What does the Biblical model have to say to us in terms of Gospel communication today?

I would respond that the Biblical model points us toward a reality. That is, the church should first be the Biblical church if it is to be a light to the world. All forms of media communication, I believe, should be servants of that more fundamental reality. I believe the Biblical model of community is a called, worshiping, and sacramentally defined community, that is, a church in the old sense of ecclesiology should be recommended over against the atomistic, individualized, solitary soul-travel of pop American evangelism. That is, we offer a unified, coherent view of reality, along with the ancient church, and I believe our missionary zeal and task are best served by being that community defined by the Bible that is also the community of truth.

We need a return to the view of ecclesiology that the early church and the Reformation church displayed, that is, wherein the worship of the community defined the consciousness of its members and its members did not think of themselves as democratic parts of a sort of voting assembly, but rather as organic parts of the living body, the Church, placed there, not by their own decision, but by sacred baptism, which incorporated them into the Body of Christ and in which they went forward then to the world, displaying the cross of Christ. It's at that level, I think, at the parish and congregational level, that we stimulate an existential, a personal, commitment to ecclesiology that imitates our forefathers. And if I could conclude with an example, the creation of a community that has this view of itself in Biblical terms and really believes with clarity and conviction that this community partakes of the reality of ultimate truth, that sort of community will by its nature, I would suggest, be missionary. Now for the example: today I have two sons who are out at their school, I'm sure, holding up the St. Louis Cardinals' victory. In fact, they stayed up late to listen to it, and, ontologically, they knew that the truth had been perceived and realized, and now they're busy displaying. Well, if that sort of motivation can come from a devotion to a sports team, I think we need to recapture the Biblical motivation, namely, that truth is expressed in the Gospel of Jesus Christ and that it can be found nowhere else. Thank you.

Dr. Preus

I'm going to speak on Number 3 and Number 2, though I don't know much about 2. Let me say something about 2 by way of introduction. That question has already been answered as far as I can answer it—What impact does communication technology have on cross-cultural ministry and missions at home and abroad? I think it was answered very well by the Rev. Schulz when he started talking about the Mormons, because there's a different culture. They speak the same language, but they're as different a culture as the people who live in Istanbul. And what Rev. Schulz said about imaging and, what I would add, posturing, is great. But the Mormons are not making their great impact by the media, as good a job as they're doing. They're making their great impact by follow-up. Maybe not by Bible classes, as he said, and information classes, such as other radio programs have, but by missionaries. I remember the first congress on evangelization at Berlin. Billy Graham said, "I'll never do it, with all the preaching, preaching, preaching." And those were the days when he and Hoffmann and a few others had it a little more to themselves. You have to have the follow-up. And I'm not even sure that follow-up by way of instructional materials will do the job. It has to be people. And the Mormons have the people. We have them, too. Roman Catholics have them in great abundance, but we're not using them, and the Roman Catholics aren't at all. So the Pope just postures and images in this country. A lot of people go out to see him and try to fall under his mantle and shadow, to get a little publicity themselves, maybe. But ultimately it will do very little in my estimation. You won't see any church growth. You won't see anything happening, because it has no follow-up. I guess I've answered the third question, too, a little bit.

I can't answer questions on culture, sub-culture, except repeat what Rev Schulz said, that the only way you can do it in a culture like China is to follow up your radio with some sort of printed word, whereby those interested and touched by the message will educate themselves. And I think that when Dr. Morris Watkins talked about statistics, he indicated that the church growth over there was accomplished not through the media, but through people. And if we can direct our media so that it can get people to follow up what the media postures and images, so that if that's all we can do through the media, it'll probably be good.

Dr. Hesselgrave

I'm going to speak on the third question: What do we need to do to make sure that God's intended message is actually communicated for understanding.

About ten-fifteen years ago, in a consultation like this at Trinity, I asked Dr. Norman Geissler, whom some of you should know and who was at that time on our faculty, to state for us from a philosophical point of view what was the first priority in cross-cultural communication and he said something to the effect that if you're talking about cross-cultural communication you're probably talking about different world-views. And from a philosophical point of view the primary thing to recognize would be that everyone has glued to their noses world-view glasses and that those glasses are very, very difficult, in fact almost painful, to take off, and therefore we have to make the adjustment. From a missionary point of view we have to bear the pain of taking off our Christian world-view glasses just long enough to put theirs on and try to see the world as they see it if we're going to communicate with them.

Another way to say this is—if we're going to communicate cross-culturally, we have to think world-viewishly. There are literally thousands of religions in the world, but they can really be narrowed down to basically five or six different world-views, such as the monistic world view of Hinduism and Buddhism, the pantheistic or panentheistic world view of many Chinese, the polytheistic world view of the animists and tribalists, the monotheistic world view of Judaism, Christianity, and Islam, the naturalistic, mechanistic, humanistic world view of secularism, and branches of these. Now when we think in these terms, when we view communication world-viewishly, at least two things are going to happen. Number one, we begin to detect areas where our own world-view is not wholly Christian. That's an important part of the exercise. Hindu-Buddhistic monism will make us rethink our tendency toward materialism, for example. Tribalism will make us reconsider the Biblical emphases on the spirit world and take them far more seriously than most of us do in our preaching, teaching, and living.

Secondly, we'll begin to see that to be meaningful, communication must be adjusted so as to make sense, be meaningful, within these alternative world-views. I remember the evangelist who was going to India, and I said, "Well, what are you going to preach on?" And he said, "What else? You must be born again." I said, "Please go some place else other than India." For Indians, that's not good news, that's horrendous news. You're reinforcing their great problem, that is, their attachment to samsara, to reincarnation. In fact, they hear this and they will say, "Oh, no, he says it, too. You've got to be born again." Well, I could give you thousands of similar examples.

Now, just a word in that connection on Biblical theology, which I mentioned yesterday. Ultimately, the framework for a Christian world-view, it seems to me, is best provided by Biblical theology. Not just theology that's Biblical, but Biblical theology. And subservience, if you will, of theological method to the revelational merit of history and eschatology. That's the most viable way of communicating a Christian world view and I think particularly in cross-cultural communication. We're going to have to start in a significant way with where the Bible starts and where the Bible ends. You can take an entry point with Christ, for example, but you immediately go back to the Word who was in the beginning. In the beginning God, and then you end with a resounding Amen to his ultimate triumph. And then you fill in that which is in between.

Now, just a word on that other question: communication in Biblical times was primarily done without technological media—what does that model have to say to us in communication today? I team-teach a course in counselling—cross-cultural counselling—with Dr. David Dillon, and I was encouraged when I first went in with him to discover that he says that all counselling begins with the discovery of the private world-view of the counselee. And since I'm greatly interested in public world-view and he's interested in private world-view, we come together at that point. Ultimately, every person is idiosyncratic; he or she speaks a private language called an idiolect; he or she has his or her own fingerprints, a privatized world-view. The significance of this is that ultimately effective communication is inter-personal—it's face-to-face. And all communication comes down comes down to that, and that's where our witness ultimately is. It can be connected with all of the media presentation and witnessed, but nothing ultimately replaces face to face communication of who Christ is, what he has done for the world, and what he's done for us.

Mr. Law

(Note: Mr. Robert C. Law is president of Christian Leaders Association, a group of international lay ministry teams. He is also founder and president of R. C. Law & Co., Inc., a publisher and distributor of Christian books located in Fullerton, California. R. C. Law & Co. has assisted The Great Commission Resource Library with the publishing of Seven Worlds to Win, Missions Resource Handbook by Dr. Morris Watkins, and The Great Commission Study Guide. He has published Unlocking the Mystery of Revelation by Pastor James Knotek. Mr. Law lives in Walnut, California. He is married and the father of four children.)

I will speak about questions four and two.

I have to differ from my colleagues, perhaps, in cross-culture. As a layman seated between Dr. Preus and Rev. Schulz, I am in a cross-cultural situation right now, and I'm in culture shock, so I hope you'll lift me as I share my responses to these questions.

Communication and community have something in common. They are both "commune" words, literally meaning "together as one." Communication cannot be effective without community. It requires togetherness as oneness. It is a dialogue. It's participation. It is involvement. It is mutual immersion in a relationship. In simplest terms, it is a two-way street. In this sense, lecturing is not communication, proclamation is not communication, even arguing is not communication, because nobody is listening. Therefore, full communication of God's message requires full communication among God's people. It is interactive, responsive, sensitive, and constructive. It requires listening. All of us as pastors or laymen must focus a great deal of energy on developing our true communicating skills. This means being responsive to the thoughts, ideas, and emotions of those about us. Not just dictating our concepts and understandings as ultimate truth.

In the videos that were shown yesterday in the Student Commons and, I might add, last night in Dr. Bunkowske's message, one common theme evident in each was the effective adaptation of the Gospel to the individual needs, character, and nature of those to whom the ministry was directed. The social, emotional, and intellectual needs of one group of people are likely to be different from those of another. These differences are distinctives of character, but not standards of quality to be measured or changed. We need to elevate, not evaluate, and we do so within a society or social structure, not generally by attempting to uproot or alter the structure itself.

To do this, we must for one thing be able to identify and associate with the subject body. A common phrase included in the covenant of many churches of various denominations affirms that we shall "walk circumspectly in the world." Though well-intended, I feel that this is a very dangerous statement, because it literally means to walk around looking in. If we walk around the world looking into it, we cannot identify with it or feel it or understand it. I question that we can communicate with it. It was certainly not the manner of communication chosen by our Lord Jesus Christ.

I do not suggest that when in Rome we must do as the Romans. I do not suggest that we have to be of the world to be in the world. But I do believe we have to: (1) enter Rome, (2) breathe in an understanding of the Roman atmosphere and nature, and (3) speak Roman. To the local pastor and layman, therefore, I would suggest: go out on the front step of your sanctuary and look at your Rome. Look intently. Walk the streets in solitude and look, listen, and even smell the neighborhood. Then, in engaging prospective communicants in conversation, emphasize your power of listening. The hardest thing to do is listen, yet it is surely one of the highest qualities of the effective parish pastor or lay minister. Then, when you speak, do it in Roman. I mean, of course, in the manner and fashion that will be best understood. All evangelical endeavor is, to some extent, cross-cultural in nature. The culture of the unsaved in a community will be as distinct from the culture of the saved as many ethnic cultural distinctions of modern times. Cross-cultural communication will be severely tested by merely communicating the Gospel with the alcoholic, the street walker, or even the atheistic professor at a local university.

But the high state of the art in communications today makes

the interrelational even more essential and more difficult. So how do you present dialogue in a printed brochure or a video tape? In effect, how do you listen when you're the only one talking? I will conclude with one part of the answer, and I might interject, as we have talked about the successes of the Mormons, this is a part of their answer. You do it by understanding your viewer or reader and presenting your message in a manner that is sensitive to his viewpoint, his culture, and his vocabulary. In effect, you are listening as you speak. You are placing yourself in his shoes. The ultimate success of modern technology does not, in my opinion, depend upon anything particularly different from the method used so effectively 2,000 years ago by that itinerant teacher from Nazareth who spoke so often in parables. Why? Because that is what his listeners would best understand. Let us use this example of our Savior as a direct model of our own communication. Can we do anything more? Thank you.

Dr. Voelz

I will speak on questions one and three.

Number one is the matter of technological communication and not being able in Bible times and today. The literary critic Walter Ong has observed that society in general, culture in general, has moved from orality to a print culture to a secondary orality. What he means by this is before the massive dissemination of the printed word, people basically communicated through speech, through story which was spoken, tales which were retold. And with the printing press, we had large dissemination, such as you could not have with handwritten manuscripts, of print, so that we became a print culture. He now observes that many people are turning away from books. In fact, there is a rise of illiteracy in our country, as you know, and people are watching videos; they are listening to audio cassette tapes; and there is a rise in what is called secondary orality so that people are now receiving their information from television or from tapes or whatever, rather than reading it.

Now, I think you can probably all resonate to this and see that it in fact is true. If it is so, Walter Ong is a reminder to us that perhaps we have the wrong distinction here. The distinction is not between technology and nontechnology; it may be between visual and oral. And if this is right, then, I think we have to rethink whether or not we are simply going from low gimmickry to high gimmickry. Are we moving, let us say, from a printed or an oral presentation of the Gospel, to a video presentation of the Gospel, in which case we have to ask ourselves are videos, let us say, doing something other than was intended in the presentation style of the Gospel as it was originally given.

I appreciated so much Mr. Law's comments. As a reader-oriented critic, his sort of reader-reception ideas are right up my alley. But the point here, I think, is that the way the Gospel can be most effectively communicated is through story, which is essentially heard, not through information, which is essentially read. I think proof of this, of course, is that this is what preaching was for Luther, and for Lutherans preaching is still such a primary thing. A little footnote here. This is why personally I totally disagree with the idea that the lessons of the Sunday morning worship should be printed in the bulletin. You should **hear** the lessons, you should not be reading along. They will have a completely different impact for you when they are heard, as they were originally designed to do.

Now, on the third point, about what needs to be done to make certain that God's intended communication is given to another culture. Here I'd have to go back to what I said about metaphor—that metaphor is not basically decorative. It is our key understanding, and it seems to me that the problem here is that when we move to different cultures, we tend to have metaphor shifts, and we also tend to have different meanings and attendant connotations of metaphors in different culture.

It's very easy for us to think that we should make the move from "I am the Good Shepherd" to "I am the pig farmer" when we move to New Guinea and to think that we simply pick metaphors which are properly available from a culture. But, as I hope I showed yesterday in the paper, metaphors have implications, and at our great peril do we change someone from being a shepherd to a pig farmer, because pigs aren't sheep and sheep aren't pigs. And so we start to have a shift in the implication of the message. Thus, we might say, if you're in North Dakota and you're not near a seacoast, perhaps we shouldn't talk about a ship of state. Maybe we should talk about the body politic. But we have a different conception of the state at that point, because a captain can and should be mutineed against if he is leading the ship aground. With a body, if you cut off the head, the body dies. Thank you.

Rev. Schulz

We'll look briefly at number 4: what can local pastors and laymen do to carry out a more full communication of God's message in their local context of ministry? As we look at this question, I would like to also pose another rhetorical question of my own. My interest in seminary days was church history; my primary interest was the Reformation. And as I studied the Reformation and the things that took place following the new preaching of the Word, I was still and remain absolutely overwhelmed at the type of missionary and evangelistic work that went on. Dioceses were changed. The Reformation and the understanding of the Gospel moved through different countries. Tremendous changes took place. So my question is—this is a question for all of us: why is it today when we have this powerful heritage and we see what has been done in the past, why are we so prone today to always run to the state fair of gimmicks to find a new methodology? I use them and have used many of them. I say this because the implication in number 4 is generally one where what kind of new program is available today?

I remember when the Kennedy program came out. I was in St. Louis by invitation in the late sixties when Dr. Kennedy, who was a personal friend of mine, made the presentation from some sheets that were run off of a mimeograph; they weren't even published. I remember that. And it came about, as it says in the Bible, you know, that things come to pass, that eventually that thing went around the country and it was one of the greatest things, that was the thing that would really bring people into the church. I learned a lot from that program. Never really used it in its fullness. But I learned certain things.

In light of these comments, I would like to say now: what can local pastors and laymen do to carry out a more full communication of God's message in the local context of the ministry. The number one thing we can do is fill the pastor's confirmation class. I've worked now for two decades in this work, different levels, and I would like somebody to convince me that there is a more effective tool for evangelism in our society today than the pastor's confirmation class. I don't know of any. And I've watched, even when the Word of God is taught. Tremendous changes. I've as I've served as a pastor, the phenomenal things that take place witnessed II Corinthians 5 come alive: Therefore, if any man is in Christ, he is a new creation. I remember a man who came there; he had been through some other courses before. He was an enthusiast for automobiles and he came there; he had a lot of rough edges and he wasn't very friendly. Today, as a result of the Word, he is a changed man. "Therefore, if any man is in Christ, he is a new creation."

Dr. Hesselgrave, I salute you. I checked out, it must have been, at least eight books before I came here. I'd never met you. Learned a lot. You're a prolific writer, and I appreciate that a lot. And what I have to say in reaction to cross-cultural work is in no way negative. Herman Sasse, who wrote the book *Here We Stand,* mentions that the Lutheran catechism in its birth, in its origin, is German. Nevertheless, that book was translated rapidly into many languages. And very effectively brought about tremendous evangelistic results. It is truly a unique world-view.

I think also, though, that when we proclaim the Gospel we must have this, and yet we must not try to adapt, and I don't think you've ever said that. We have to preach the Word and have total confidence in it. Let me give you an illustration. I suppose some of you think that I am a little critical here, and I suppose that I am. Does the Lutheran Hour work? Well, what can I say? Let me give you an example. We have one transmitter in the country of Jamaica. That's certainly cross-cultural. It's a secular station. I was there for a conference two years ago. I was sitting in the back. It was terribly hot. It was late at night and I was about falling to sleep, as most people do that attend meetings such as this today. A man tapped me on the shoulder, and he said to me, "Will you come outside?" He said, "I'm president of a local pastors' alliance and I want to tell you that our radio station here in Kingston is the most widely-listened-to radio station in the whole country, and your program, The Lutheran Hour, is second." There is not a Lutheran church in the whole country. Our aggregate mail count for the Lutheran Hour several years ago was 23,000 pieces of mail. As anybody knows, this is staggering. I was in a meeting in New York City not long ago, and a couple of broadcasters were there and they cornered me right away. They wondered how we do this. Well, I said, we preach the Gospel. We don't say, if you do this, God will do this. We announce total pardon, total pardon to those who will listen.

If I can end with this little example, Dr. Bunkowske, I have to say this in the total context of what we're doing. We get literally fistfuls of mail, fistfuls, and I would be glad to share them with you, letters from people who write us and who say, "I believe in Jesus, I trust in Jesus, I have faith in Jesus, but I'm not a Christian." I've been to many of these countries myself and preached there in many different ways, and I've come to learn that is the product of what is called the most damnable type of thing that's done among Christians and that is legalistic preaching. Which is to say, you straighten up your life, you clean up the act, you stop cursing and smoking and all these things and get ready to become a Christian. We go out with great boldness, great boldness; there is nothing worse than legalism. It's a terrible, damnable thing, spoken clearly against by Paul in Galatians 1:7-8. If we add one iota to the Gospel, to what Jesus cried out on Good Friday, "It is finished,"—that's legalism. We go ahead with the media in the hope and the power of the Gospel, in line with Galatians 3:23-25, that people might be let out of prison.